Marketing and Sustainable Development

Marketing and Sustainable Development

Pooja Saxena

RAWAT PUBLICATIONS
Jaipur and New Delhi

Published by
Prem Rawat for ***Rawat Publications***
Satyam Apts., Sector 3, Jain Temple Road, Jawahar Nagar, Jaipur - 4 (India)
Phone: 0141 651748 / 657006 Fax: 0141 651748
e-mail : info@rawatbooks.com
www.rawatbooks.com

Delhi Office
G-4, 4832/24, Ansari Road, Daryaganj, New Delhi 110 002
Phone: 011-3263290

Typeset by Rawat Computers, Jaipur
Printed at Chaman Enterprises, New Delhi

Contents

Preface

Marketing is concerned with the channels of distribution through which goods move from producers to consumers. The entire process of marketing is performed at places known as 'market centres'; which as organisms, are not passive mechanical phenomena contributing to a geometric pattern spread out upon the earth's surface, but are rather active with fixed functions, behavioural patterns and growth processes. The various facets of marketing have been studied both by economists and geographers, but their relationship with ecological complex has not been studied in detail. The present volume is based on intensive field work and unfolds the role of ecological factors in growth and development of the marketing system. In other words, it deals with marketing and sustainable development.

In all, there are nine chapters in this book, starting with an Introduction, which deals with nature and scope of the study, methodology and a review of selected works done by foreign and Indian geographers. The ecological framework of the Central Hadaoti region and growth of markets in relation to the ecological complex have been explained in Chapters 2 and 3, while urban, agricultural and rural marketing patterns have been discussed in the following three chapters. A detailed analysis of the behavioural pattern of market-place participants has also been done, which is very useful for planning. Finally, in the last two chapters the impact of marketing on the environment, and problems of and planning for sustainable development have been discussed. Tables, maps and diagrams have been provided throughout the text for proper analysis. Apart from references at the end of each chapter, a detailed bibliography has also been given at the end of the book.

I express my heartfelt gratitude to my father Dr. H.M. Saxena, an eminent geographer and now Joint Director, College Education Rajasthan, Jaipur, for proper guidance, support, inspiration as well as blessings. I am also thankful to Dr. K.P. Sharma, Head, Geography Department, Government College, Beawar, for his co-operation and good wishes. Right from the beginning my mother has encouraged me to complete this work in time. My sister Dr. Deepa and brother-in-law Dr. Yogesh have also given me full support and inspiration. My thanks are also due to all those officials and non-officials who have, in some way or other, helped me in writing this book. Finally, I am thankful to Rawat Publications for the timely publication of this book.

Pooja Saxena

Chapter 1

Introduction

The present study is related with the geography of marketing, which has received considerable attention by geographers, both foreign and Indian, during the latter half of the 20th century. Marketing geography, a branch of economic geography, seeks its *raison d'etre* as a specialised study of the market-places and marketing. Applebaum (1954: 246) has defined marketing geography as being "concerned with the channels of distribution through which goods move from producers to consumers". The market-place and marketing form the core of marketing geography. The word 'market', derived from the Latin word *marcatus* refers to a place where buyers and sellers meet. Markets are spatial units. Thus, their location, site and morphology are of significance to geographers. Market centres, as organisms are not passive mechanical phenomena contributing to a geometric pattern spread out upon the earth's surface, but are rather active with fixed functions, behavioural patterns and growth processes. Their activity can be seen in the form of marketing, a process of interaction among producers, distributors, buyers and users, or in other words, it includes all processes and services through which goods move from producers to consumers.

The present study is significant because it deals with the relationship between the ecological complex and patterns of marketing. An ecological complex is a system of four interrelated clusters of variables, viz., environment, population, technology and organisation. The physical environment of a region is a determining factor for the growth of population, which is also responsible for the development of social and cultural environments. Technological innovations not only direct but determine the state of the utilisation of environmental resources and also growth of organisations—social as well as economic. Economic organisation is of prime importance for regional development. Agriculture, mining, industries and transportation are the basic components of an economic organisation, which lead to the formation and growth of market centres. Thus, market centres are the key components of economic organisation. An effective marketing system is necessary for regional economic development. The present study deals with the role of ecological factors in the growth and development of marketing systems and market-places in the Central Hadaoti region of Rajasthan State.

In the field of marketing geography several studies have been made both by foreign and Indian geographers, of various facets of markets and/or marketing. But the only study of marketing with ecological components has been done by Symanski and Bromley (1974: 382-88) in their research paper entitled "Market Development and Ecological Complex", which deals with the study of Andean markets. Therefore, the present study is first of its kind because it unfolds the environmental factors responsible for the growth of markets and marketing, and also shows the impact of marketing activity on environment.

OBJECTIVES

The main objectives of the present study are as follows:

(1) to explain the ecological framework of Central Hadaoti in terms of environment, population and socio-economic organisation;
(2) to study the relationship between growth of marketing systems with ecological variables;
(3) to study the urban marketing pattern and its structure;
(4) to describe in detail the rural marketing pattern in terms of weekly markets and fairs;
(5) to explain the agricultural marketing pattern in the region;
(6) to examine the impact of marketing activities on the environment;
(7) to study the problems of marketing in the region; and
(8) to suggest a strategy for development which is ecologically sustainable.

SOURCE OF DATA AND METHODOLOGY

Like any geographical study, the present work has been carried out with the help of three principal sources, viz.: (i) maps, statistics and available written literature; (ii) direct observation of the phenomena associated with the informants engaged in marketing activity; and (iii) interview with the informants engaged in marketing activity in the region under study.

The study has been largely based on field work and analyses of primary and secondary data. Since data regarding periodic markets and rural marketing are not available, the primary data have been collected with the help of questionnaires. Similarly, data regarding behavioural patterns of market-place participants have also been collected with the help of questionnaires.

The empirical study has been done in the field to examine the impact of marketing on environment. The secondary data have been obtained from official sources like the Statistical Department, Census Department, Rajasthan State Agricultural Marketing Board, Mandi Committees, Town Planning Department, etc.

All the collected data have been tabulated and maps and diagrams have been prepared through suitable cartographical techniques. Wherever necessary statistical techniques have also been used. For intensive study samples have been selected adopting the random sampling method. Finally, critical analysis has been done to suggest measures for sustainable development of marketing activity in the region.

HYPOTHESIS AND KEY QUESTIONS

The following hypothesis and key questions have been tested and/or discussed:

(1) The growth and development of markets is a reflection of ecological adjustment, and the existence of various forms of marketing is due to regional environmental conditions.

(2) The primary requirement of market location is the availability of road transportation.

(3) The growth of agricultural markets is the result of: (a) agricultural productivity, (b) easy accessibility, and (c) density of rural population.

(4) Farmers used to visit their nearest market for the disposal of their farm products.

(5) 'Proximity in space implies separation in time' (Fagerland and Smith, 1970).

(6) That consumers will always visit the nearest shopping centre that offers required goods and services.

(7) That all shopping trips are multi-functional in nature.

(8) That market regulation is more beneficial to farmers than traders.

(9) That markets are synchronised so as to enable the traders to follow the routes which minimise their weekly travel cost (Trader hypothesis, Smith, 1971).

(10) That markets are synchronised so as to enable the consumers to have easiest possible access to market throughout the week (Consumer hypothesis, Smith, 1971).

(11) The more the marketing activity, the more will be its impact on environment.

THE REGION

The Central Hadaoti region (24°32′ to 25°53′ N and 75°36′ to 76°35′ E) is a distinct historico-geographical region and a part of the Hadaoti Plateau covering the Kota district of Rajasthan. The total area of the region is 5,198 sq.kms. and according to the 1991 census its total population was 12,20,505. This region is a high plain area drained by the river Chambal and its main tributary Kalisindh. The region is a riverian tract having an average elevation of 300 metres above mean-sea-level. The Mukandwara hills are located in the south-eastern part of the region. The physiography, climate, natural vegetation and soil characteristics of the region provide the area with a sort of physical homogeneity which is reflected in its human geography.

REVIEW OF SELECTED WORKS

Marketing geography as an independent branch of economic geography has developed systematically only after 1950. The need for marketing geography was first pointed out by William Applebaum, an American geographer. He argued that the study of marketing had been neglected by geographers up to that time, in spite of large sections of the working population engaged in marketing functions, and a large part of urban landscape devoted to structures of wholesale and retail trade, and the complex channels of distribution leading from the producing to consuming areas (Applebaum, 1954: 246).

The practical importance of marketing geography in its initial stage has also been pointed out by other American geographers such as Saul Cohen, Howard Green and Bart Epsteen. With the growing interest among geographers, in 1961, Remond Murphy introduced a special edition of a leading

American journal, *Economic Geography* entitled, 'Marketing Geography Comes of Age'. Its separate status was recognised by the International Geographical Union (IGU) only in 1972 at the time of the 22nd IGU Congress at Montreal, when a working group on 'Market-Place Exchange Systems' was constituted. The working group has done commendable work from 1972 to 1984 under the co-chairmanship of Professors R.H.T. Smith and E. Gromsen. A new study group, 'Geography of Commercial Activities' was formed in 1984 with Prof. A. Metton as its chairman. This study group was soon converted into an IGU commission in 1988. Prof. V.K. Srivastava of Gorakhpur University was the chairman of this commission for a period of three years. In 1996, at the Hague IGU session, another study group on 'Globalisation of Retailing' was created under the chairmanship of Prof. A Metton (France). In fact, during the last four decades, marketing geography has received considerable attention both from foreign and Indian geographers. The literature available on marketing geography is vast and it is not possible to highlight all. A brief review of the work done by foreign and Indian geographers has been given here.

Contribution by Foreign Geographers

Among foreign publications, Berry's (1967) book *Geography of Market Centres and Retail Distribution* is a pioneering work dealing with retailing, delineation and measuring of trading area. The other notable books are *Marketing Geography* (Davies, 1976), *Geography of Marketing* (Garnier and Delobez, 1979) and *Geography of Marketing and Urban Growth* (Mulvihill and Mulvihill, 1976). Peter Scott's (1970) book *Geography of Retailing* and James E.Vance Jr.'s (1970) book *The Merchants World: The Geography of Wholesaling* are also notable contributions in this field. All these books have given a solid base to the field of marketing geography.

The origin of market-places has been discussed by Hodder (1974). The distribution of market centres in Yorubaland and United States has been described by Hodder (1965) and Pyle (1971). The origin of markets in relation to ecology has been explain by Symanski and Bromley (1974). Proudfoot (1937) was the first who has described the market morphology and its components with reference to American cities. Weimer and Hoyt (1940), Brown and Davidson (1953), Kelley (1955) and Berry (1967) have discussed the morphology and infrastructures of the market centres. Davies (1976) has classified the shopping centres of British towns.

Several geographical studies have been made to explain the market area or market sphere of influence. Reilly's *Law of Retail Gravitation* (1937) modified by Converse (1949) and Huff (1963) are the classical works. Other works based on gravity models have been done by Lakshmanan and Hanson (1965), Renyolds (1953), Riddell (1961) and Carruther (1963). Ullman (1960) has used traffic flow as basis of determining the market area. Several other studies of market area based on 'Central Place Theory', are included in the classic works of Christaller (1933) and Losche (1940) followed by Berry (1967). The notable studies related to consumer behaviour have been done by Berry, Barnum and Tennant (1962), Davies (1973), Hortan (1968) and Huff (1969).

Geographers have paid much attention to the study of periodic markets. The various facets of periodic markets like origin, spatio-temporal synchronisation, periodicity, morphology, commodity structure, market cycles, etc., have been studied in detail. The relationship between temporal and locational spacing was discussed by Hodder and Ukwu (1969), Fagerland and Smith (1970), Smith (1970), Wood (1978) and Bromley (1976). This relationship has also been examined in terms of trader and consumer hypothesis by Smith (1971), Smith and Hay (1969), Gana (1976), etc. Periodicity is an important aspect of these markets and has been studied by Good (1973), Hodder (1971), Smith (1971) and Bromley (1975), etc. Market cycles have been explained by Hodder (1961), Thomas (1924), Polaman (1961), Hill (1966) and Alao (1968). The hierarchy of periodic markets has been examined by Skinner (1964), Berry (1961), C.A. Smith (1976) and Bromley (1974).

Another institution of periodic marketing is the fair. As early as in 1919, Wrigley's article on 'Fairs of Central Andes' was published in *Geographical Review*. The other works on fairs have been published by Allix (1922), Spencer (1940), Hodgen (1942), Kniffan (1949), Hodder and Sinha (1976). In comparison to weekly markets lesser geographical studies of fairs has been done during the past few decades.

Indian Contribution

Indian geographers have made a significant contribution in the field of marketing geography during the last three decades. After 1970 several studies have been conducted by geographers in the universities of Udaipur, Gorakhpur, Madras, Madurai, Kanpur, Nagpur, Allahabad, Jabalpur and Banaras on themes related with marketing in their regional setting. This was the real beginning of marketing geography, although prior to it several research papers had been published on themes related to marketing geography. Indian geographers have also made substantial contribution in the IGU study group commission on 'Market-place Exchange Systems' and 'Geography of Commercial Activities'. Under the Chairmanship of Prof. Srivastava (Gorakhpur) several international and national conferences have been organised at Gorakhpur, Pokhara (Nepal), Dhaka (Bangladesh) and New Delhi during 1994-95. These conferences have given an opportunity to young geographers of India not only to present their research findings but also to undertake further research in the field of marketing geography. The contributions made by V.K. Srivastava, Tamaskar, H.M. Saxena, Wanmali, Dixit, Jayshankar and

Gedam are notable in this field. Barbara Harris, H. Ishihara, H.G. Bhole and E.A.J. Johnson are the foreign geographers who have worked in India and have contributed significantly.

A survey of the geographical research in the field of marketing reveals that Indian geographers have contributed on the following themes:

(i) Theoretical and methodological studies,
(ii) Origin, classification and typology of market centres,
(iii) Urban/daily markets,
(iv) Periodic/rural markets (weekly markets and fairs),
(v) Role of market centres in development and planning.

The detail of works done by Indian geographers for regions located in India, tabulated by Saxena in his unpublished report on 'Geography of Commercial Activities in India' is given here, which covers the entire contribution of Indian geographers in the field of marketing geography:

MARKETING GEOGRAPHY
Contribution by Indian Geographers/Studies related to India

S.No.	*Name of Scholar*	*Theoretical & Methodological*	*Origin Classification & Typology*	*Urban/Daily Market*	*Rural Periodic Markets*	*Agricultural/ Regulated Markets*	*Role in Development and Social aspects*	*General Case Studies*
1.	Agrawal, P.C.				*			
2.	Alam, S.M.			*	*			
3.	Andrede, C.P. & Johnson A. A.					*		
4.	Arunachalam, B.				*			
5.	Aherwadkar, L.J.					*		
6.	Bawa, R.L. & Others						*	
7.	Bedkar, S.L.					*		
8.	Bumb, B.L.					*		

Contd...

Contd...

9.	Bhole, H.G.				***	*		
10.	Bhattacharya, B.N.							*
11.	Bhowmik, K.L. & Choudhary, K.K.				*			
12.	Chandran, K.				*			
13.	Chatterjee, A.B.			*				
14.	Dass, T.K.						*	
15.	Deshpande, C.D.				*			
16.	Dutt, A.K.			**				
17.	Dayal, P. & Thakur, B.			*				
18.	De, J.			*				
19.	De, N.K.						*	
20.	Duggal, S.L.					*		
21.	Dixit, R.S.	**	***	***	*******		**	
22.	Dwivedi, S.	*						
23.	Fox, R.G.	*			*			
24.	Garg, P.K.							*
25.	Ghosh, A.						*	
26.	Gedam, D.A.				******			
27.	Geetha, T.				*			
28.	Harriss, Barbara			*	*	******		
29.	Hashim, S.R.							*
30.	Hirt, H.F.		*					
31.	Hugar, S.L.					**		
32.	Hussain, S.A.					*		
33.	Ishihara, H.				****			
34.	Johnson, E.A.J.					*	*	
35.	Jasdanualla, Z.Y.					*		
36.	Jamkar, A.G.				**			
37.	Jamuna, K.				*			
38.	Jana, M.M.			**				
39.	Jayshankar, D.C.	*					*	
40.	Jayaswal, S.N.P.		*					
41.	Kahlon, S.S. & Kehal, H.S.					*		

Contd...

Contd...

42.	Karwe, I. & Acharya, H.			*			
43.	Katiyar, R.C.			**			
44.	Khan, W.						*
45.	Khandwe, M.A.	*					
46.	Krishna, G. & Agarwal, S.K.		*				
47.	Krishan, G.			*			
48.	Krishnamurthy, B.			*			
49.	Krishna, V.			*			***
50.	Kulkarni, K.M.		*				
51.	Kulkarni, K.R.				*		
52.	Kumar, A. & Sharma, N.			*			
53.	Kumar, S.		**				
54.	Kumawat, B.L.		*				
55.	Lumbhar, A.P.			**			
56.	Lal, H. & Yadav, H.R.		*				
57.	Lal, R.S.		*				
58.	Lal, V.N.		*				*
59.	Lele, Uma, J.				***		
60.	Lessinger, J.M.				*		
61.	London, P.A.					*	
62.	Maidamwar, G.T.			*			
63.	Maikap, P.T.					*	
64.	Maishe, P.T.			*			
65.	Mandal, H.		*				
66.	Mathur, R.S.						*
67.	Mathur, V.S.				*		
68.	Mehta, I.			*			
69.	Menon, K.P.A.				*		
70.	Moore, J.R. etc.				*		
71.	Mukerji, A.B.			*			*
72.	Mukhopadhyaya, T.S.			*			
73.	Murthy, A.N.K.				*		

Contd...

Contd...

74.	Miltenderj, H.J.			*			
75.	Mohanty, S.K.		*				
76.	Mukerjee, M.		*				
77.	Mukerjee, S.P.		*				
78.	Murugesan, N. & Others			*			
79.	Muthiah, C.				*		
80.	Nandkarni, M.V.				*		
81.	Nageshwari, S. etc.			*			
82.	Narayan, B.S.,						
83.	Nath, T. & Kushwaha, R.K.				*		
84.	Nath, V.		*	*			
85.	NCAER					*****	
86.	Neale, W. et.al.		*				
87.	Nizamuddin			**	***		
88.	Parvathi, C.		***			*	
89.	Prakash Rao, V.L.S.						*
90.	Pattanaik, N.			*			
91.	Paul, M.S.						*
92.	Panniah, J.S.				*		
93.	Prasad, I.	*					
94.	Punja, H.G.				*		
95.	Raju, V.T. & Others				***		
96.	Ram, U.	*		*			
97.	Ramachandran, H.		*				
98.	Ramachandran, K.C.				**		
99.	Ramachandran, N.			*			
100.	Ramaswami, G. etc.			*			
101.	Rao, K.V.S. et.al.				**		
102.	Rao, M.S.		*				
103.	Rao, P.P., Rao, T.R.	*					

Contd...

Contd...

104.	Rao, R.P. etc.					*	
105.	Rao, R.					*	
106.	Rani, Parveen					*	
107.	Rathore, N.S.					*	
108.	Raza, M.				*		
109.	Reddy, N.V.					*	
110.	Reddy, S.N.					*	
111.	Sami, A.	*		******			
112.	Saharia, R.B. etc.			*			
113.	Sakar, A.K.					*	
114.	Saxena, H.M.	*****		******	****	***	**
115.	Selvam, L.G.					*	
116.	Shantha, Kumari				*		
117.	Sharma, N.			*			
118.	Sharma, P.K.			*			
119.	Sharma, R.C.						*
120.	Sharma, S.K.					*	
121.	Shukla, S.K.						*
122.	Sinha, A.J.					*	
123.	Singh, D.K. & Routray, R.K.				*		
124.	Singh, J.			*			
125.	Singh, J.P.			**			
126.	Singh, K.N.			*	*		
127.	Singh, L.R.				*	*	
128.	Singh, L.R. & Others		*	*	*	*	*
129.	Singh, M.				*		
130.	Singh, R.L. & Singh, R.P.M.				*		
131.	Singh, S.M.	*			*		
132.	Singh, U.			**			
133.	Sinha, D.P.						**
134.	Sinha, M.K.			*			
135.	Sinha, S.				*		

Contd...

Contd...

No.	Name							
136.	Sinha, V.N.P. & Mandal, R.B.			*				
137.	Sita, K.				*			
138.	Shivamurthy, A.				*			
139.	Srivastava, H.O.				****			
140.	Srivastava, K.R.	*			****			
141.	Srivastava, R.C.				**			
142.	Srivastava, V.K.	*****		***	***	*	**	**
143.	Srivastava, V.K. & Others				***			
144.	Swaminathan, E.			**	**			
145.	Singhal, K.S.				*			
146.	Subbiah, S.				*			
147.	Talwar, B.R.					*		
148.	Tamaskar, B.G.	*			******** **			*
149.	Thakur, B.			**				
150.	Tiwari, R.C. & Lal, M.				**			
151.	Twade, M.D. & Gophane B.N.					*		
152.	Verma, L.N. & Saxena, H.M.			*				
153.	Vasudeo, Rao D.				*			
154.	Venugopal, V.			*				
155.	Verma, R.D.				*			
156.	Verma, D.V.				*			
157.	Vishwanath, M.S.							**
158.	Vishwanath, V.V.					**		
159.	Wanmali, S.	*			****	**	**	
160.	Yadav, R.S.		*		*		*	

It becomes clear from the above survey that in India, marketing geography has now attained a status of specialised field of research. Under ICSSR and UGC financial assistance programme several geographers have completed major and minor research projects in the field of marketing geography.

In Rajasthan, the first notable research work has been done by H.M. Saxena for his Ph.D. at University of Udaipur. His work, *Transport and Market Centres of Hadaoti Plateau* (1971 published in 1975) is the first of its kind. Kumawat (1973) and H.S. Rathore (1979) have presented the analysis of market towns of Central Aravalli and Rajasthan respectively. The ICSSR research projects completed by Saxena on 'Rural Markets in Rajasthan', 'Regulated Agricultural Markets in Rajasthan' and 'Behavioural Pattern of Market-Place Participants: A Regional Analysis of Rajasthan' are notable works. Retail Marketing at Jaipur was studied by B.L. Gupta, while R.S. Yadav, Gursimran Kaur, Parveen Rani and K.P. Sharma have done Ph.D. works related with marketing geography.

On marketing geography, bibliographies compiled by Ray Bromley (1974, 1979) and Waine Mckim (1985) and review articles by Saxena (1977), Srivastava (1984) and Dixit (1997) provide detailed information of the works done by foreign and Indian geographers.

COVERAGE

The present research work unfolds the market ecology of the Central Hadaoti region. The study has been divided into nine chapters. A brief chapter-wise analysis is given below.

Chapter 1 is an introductory chapter dealing with the nature and scope of the study, objectives, methodology and review of selected works done by foreign and Indian geographers. The review reveals that enough work has been done in the field of marketing geography but so far detailed study of markets and marketing has not been done with its relation to ecological framework of the region. Therefore, the present study is important.

The ecological framework of the region has been described in chapter 2. It deals with (i) geographical environment, (ii) demographic structure, and (iii) economic and social organisation. The Central Hadaoti region embodies a distinct geographical individuality in terms of physiography, climate, natural vegetation, soil and water bodies. The ecosystem of the region is very much controlled by the physical environment. The Central Hadaoti region is a riverian tract drained by river Chambal and its tributaries. Climatically, the region enjoys a sub-tropical 'monsoon' climate with seasonal variations in temperature and rainfall. According to the 1991 census, the total population of Kota district was 12,20,505. In the region 50.53 per cent population is urban distributed in seven urban centres, in which Kota is the largest town having 5,37,371 population in 1991. The percentage of SC and ST population was 20.97 and 9.10 respectively in 1991.

The economic structure of the region is dominated by agriculture. The region is a good producer of rice, jowar, maize, wheat, gram, barley, rape and mustard, linseed and soyabean. The irrigation facilities are available through canals of the Chambal system as well as from tube and other wells. The region is rich in building stone. Kota is the largest industrial centre not only of the region but of the state. The region also has good rail and road network. The present social system of the region is the outcome of a long play of factors—historical and economic.

Since it was a part of a single princely state social homogeneity can be seen throughout the region. The ecological framework of the region has provide a base for regional development including the development of marketing activities.

Chapter 3 deals with growth of markets and ecological complex. The regional ecological framework plays a vital role in growth of markets and marketing and is also responsible for spatial-linkages both inter and intra-markets. The growth of marketing in the Central Hadaoti region has been described during ancient, medieval and modern periods. Finally, the relationship between marketing system and markets and the ecological complex has been explained.

'Urban Markets and Marketing' is the theme of chapter 4. In Central Hadaoti eight market towns identified are Kota,

Ramganjmandi, Sangod, Kaithoon, Suket, Itawa, Sultanpur and Sumerganjmandi. The spatial distribution and location of market towns have been examined in relation to (i) transportation, (ii) market towns as 'break-of-bulk' centres, (iii) agricultural land use, and (iv) surrounding villages and population. The urban market morphology and infrastructures have been described on the basis of morphological components and a case study of Kota has been done in order to explain the morphological structure of an urban market. The wholesale and retail marketing pattern in urban marketing has also been explained.

An important aspect of marketing is the agricultural marketing through which farm products move from producer to the consumer. The various facets of agricultural marketing have been discussed in chapter 5. The process and pattern of agricultural marketing growth of regulated marketing, market yards and infrastructures and commodity structures have been analysed with a regional perspective. In Central Hadaoti five regulated markets exist. Kota is the 'Super A' class *mandi*, followed by 'A' class at Ramganjmandi. Sumerganjmandi, Itawa and Sangod are B, C and D class *mandis*. The role of regulated markets in rural development has also been discussed.

Chapter 6 entitled 'Pattern of Rural Marketing' deals with nature and types of rural marketing in the region under study. Periodic markets are the main rural marketing institutions in Central Hadaoti region. The weekly markets and fairs both are periodic in nature and provide marketing facilities to rural masses. In the region weekly markets (hats or hatwara) are held at 25 places. The distribution, periodicity, market cycle, internal organisation, layout, commodity structure and marketing process in weekly markets have been discussed in detail. The fair known as 'mela' are held once or twice in a year and provide marketing opportunities to the rural masses. The origin, distribution, schedule and periodicity, types and marketing in fairs have been described. In all, 48 fairs are held in Central Hadaoti region.

Chapter 7, titled 'Behavioural Pattern of Market-Place Participants' is a new dimension of research in marketing geography. On the basis of detailed field work consumer behaviour in urban markets, trader-consumer behaviour in periodic markets and producer, seller and traders' behaviour in regulated agricultural markets have been analysed in detail. The behavioural pattern of market-place participants varies according to socio-economic factors like income, level of literacy, nature of demand, status, mode of transport, specialisation of market, behaviour of shopkeepers, etc.

The impact of marketing activity on the environment has been examined in chapter 8 of the thesis. The impact of marketing on local environment has been discussed both in urban and rural areas. The urban marketing system is responsible for traffic congestion, unplanned growth as well as for air and noise pollution. The problem of waste disposal has also been created by marketing activities. These problems are more at Kota because other towns are too small. In agricultural mandis problems like air pollution has also been created by marketing activity. Similarly in rural areas the impact of weekly markets and fairs on environment can be seen. But since these are periodic in nature, their impact is also temporary in nature.

The final chapter has been devoted to the problems and planning for sustainable development.

The present study not only explains the role of ecological factors in growth and development of marketing system and/or market centres in Central Hadaoti but also paves the way for sustainable development. The study also reveals that periodic marketing is a suitable commercial activity, specially for the rural areas because these markets are economically viable, ecologically sound and socially acceptable. In fact, periodic markets are ecologically sustainable. Therefore, due attention should be given to their proper functioning and development.

There is a need for an integrated approach in planning of the marketing activities and efforts should be made for long term planning.

References

Beaujeu Garnier, J. & Delobez, A., (1979), *Geography of Marketing*, Longman, London.

Berry, B.J.L. (1967), *Geography of Market Centres and Retail Distribution*, Prentice Hall.

Bhole, H.G. (1979), Socio-Economic Characteristics and Mobility Patterns of Weekly Market Participants in Coastal Tamilnadu, *Bombay Geographical Magazine*, Vol. 27, pp. 5-21.

Bromley, R.J. (1971), Markets in the Developing Countries: A Review, *Geography*, Vol. 56, pp. 124-32.

— (1973), The Spatial Pattern and Temporal Synchronization of Periodic Markets, *Swansea Geographer*, Vol. 12, pp. 15-215.

--- (1974), *Periodic Markets, Daily Markets and Fairs: A Bibliography*, Monash University Publications in *Geography*, No. 10.

--- (1979), *Periodic Markets, Daily Markets and Fairs*, A Bibliography Supplement to 1979, Centre for Development Studies, University College of Swansea.

Cook, Scott and Diskin, M. (eds.) (1975), *Markets in Oaxaca*, University of Texas Press, Austin, p. 329.

Davies, R.L. (1976), *Marketing Geography*, Methuen, London.

Dixit, R.S., (1984), *Market Centres and their Spatial Development in the Umland of Kanpur*, Kitab Mahal, Allahabad.

--- (1997), Development of Marketing Geography India, *Geographical Review of India*, Vol. 59, No. 2, pp. 164-172.

Gana, J.A. (1976), The Locational Pattern and Functions of Periodic Markets in Zeria Division, *Nigeria Savanna*, Vol. 5, pp. 163-74.

Good, C.M. (1972), Periodic Markets: A Problem in Locational Analysis, *Professional Geographer*, Vol. 24, p. 210-14.

Harriss, B. (1976), Social Specificity in Rural Weekly Markets: The Case of Northern Tamilnadu, India, in Gormsen, E., (ed.) *Market Distribution System*. Mainger Geographiche Studiesn, No.10, Mainz, pp. 39-48.

Hodder, B.W. (1961), Rural Periodic Day Markets in Part of *Yorubaland, Transactions of the Institute of British Geographers,* No. 29, pp. 149-59.

---- (1965), Some Comments on the Origins of Traditional Markets in Africa South of Sahara, *Transactions of the Institute of British Geographers*, No. 36, pp. 97-105.

--- (1965), Distribution of Markets in Yorubaland, *Scottish Geographical Magazine*, Vol. 81, pp. 48-58.

---- (1970), Traditional Markets in Developing Countries, pp. 106-9 in 21st IGU Congress 1968 Selected Papers. Vol. 2, *Economic Geography*, Calcutta.

---- and Lee, R. (1974), *Economic Geography*, Methuen, London (esp. pp. 135-47).

Ishihara, H. (1982), Markets in East Central China during the Ming, Ching and Minkuo Period, in *Market Place Exchange Systems: Empirical and Theoretical Studies*, edited by Brarnsen, E. and Smith R.H.T., Mainz, pp. 34-43.

---- (1983), Distribution of Markets in India and Bangladesh, *The Journal of the Faculty of Literature*, Nagoya University, Vol. 83, (in Japanese with English abstract).

---- (ed.) (1987), *Markets and Marketing in Rural Bangladesh*, Department of Geography, Faculty of Letters, Nagoya University, p. 211.

Johnson, J. and Wanmali, S. (1981), An Analysis of Periodic Market System, *Geography Analysis*, Vol. 13, No. 3, pp. 262-275.

Mukerji, A.B. (1955), Economic Trends in the Market of Central Birbhum, *Geographical Review of India*, Vol. 17. No.2.

Mulvihill, D.F. and Mulvihill, R.C. (1967), *Geography Marketing and Urban Growth*, Van, Nostrand Reinhold, New York.

Norton, A., and Symanski, R. (1975), The Internal Marketing System of Jamaica, *Geographical Review*, Vol. 65 pp. 461-75.

Obaudho, R.A. (1984), The Role of Periodic and Daily Markets in Planning from Below in Africa: Towards a New Spatial

Development Strategy, Presented to 35th IGC Symposium, No. 16, *Market Place Exchange System*, August 1984.

Plattner, S.M. (1975), Rural Market Networks, *Scientific American*, Vol. 232, No. 5, pp. 66-69.

Preston, Lee E. (1970), Marketing Organisation and Economic Development Structure, Products and Management, in Bucklin, L.P. (ed.) *Vertical Marketing Systems*, Scott Proesman and Co, Glencoe, Illinois, pp. 116-134.

Saxena, H.M. (1972), *Regulated Agriculture Markets*, Rawat Publications, Jaipur.

---- (1975), *Geography of Transport and Market Centres: A Case Study of Hadaoti Plateau*, S. Chand and Co. New Delhi, p. 211.

---- (1983), Rural Markets: A Perspective for Development *Annals of the Association of Rajasthan Geographers*, Vol. 1, No. 1 & 2, pp. 19-2.

--- (1988), *Rural Markets and Development*, Rawat Publications, Jaipur.

Srivastava, V.K. (1983), Morphology of the Rural Markets around Gorakhpur Town, *The Indian Journal of Marketing Geography*, Vol. 1, pp. 28-38.

---- (1984), Progress of Marketing Geography in India, *The Indian Journal of Marketing Geography*, Vol.. II, No. 1 & 2, pp. 1-13.

--- (ed.) (1988), *Commercial Activities and Rural* Development in South Asia: A Geographical Approach, Concept, New Delhi.

Singh, L.R. (1983), *Spatial Planning of Rural Markets in India*, Vol. 18, No. 2, pp. 193-204.

Singh, S.M. (1965), The Stability Theory of Rural Central Place Development, *National Geographical Journal of India*, Vol. 11, Part-1, pp. 13-21.

Skinner, G.W. (1964), Marketing and Social Structure in Rural China I, II, III, *Journal of Asian Studies*, Vol. 24, pp. 3-43. (1965) Vol. 24, pp. 195-228 and (1965) Vol. 24, pp. 363-99.

Smith, C.A. (1974), Economics of Marketing Systems: Models from Economic Geography, *Annual Review of Anthropology*, Vol. 3, pp. 167-201.

--- (1976), *Regional Analysis, Academic Press*, New York, 2 Vols.

Smith, R.H.T. (1971), West African Market Places: Temporal Periodicity and Locational Spacing, in Millassoux, C. (ed.) *The*

Development of Indigenous Trade and markets in West Africa. Oxford University, Press, London, pp. 319-46.

— (1979), Periodic Market-Places and Periodic Marketing: Review and Prospects-I, *Progress in Human Geography*, Vol. 3, No. 4, pp. 471-505.

--- and Hay, A.M. (1969), A Theory of Spatial Structure of Internal Trade in Underdeveloped Countries, *Geographical Analysis*, Vol. 1, pp. 121-36.

Stine, J.H. (1962), Temporal Aspects of Tertiary Production Elements in Korea, in Pitts, F.R. (ed.) *Urban Systems and Economic Development*, University of Oregon, Oregon.

Symanski, R., and Bromley, R. (1974), Market Development and the Ecological Complex, *Professional Geographer*, Vol., 26, pp. 382-88.

Tamaskar, B.G. (1966), The Weekly Markets of the Sagar Damoh Plateau, *National Geographical Journal of India*, Vol. 12, No. 1, March, pp. 38-50.

— (1978), Geographic Perspective on Periodic Marketing Systems and Network in the Chattisgarh Plain, *Geographical Review of India*, Vol. 40, No. 1. pp. 15-24.

Verma, L.N. and Saxena H.M. (1968), Jhalrapatan: A Geographical Study of a Market Centre, *Deccan Geographer*, Vol. 6, No. 2, pp. 25-34.

Wanmali, S. (1980), The Regulated and Periodic Markets and Rural Development in India, *Institute of British Geographers Transactions*, Vol. 5, No. 4, pp. 456/486.

--- (1981), *Periodic Markets and Rural Development in India*, B.R. Pub. Corporation, Delhi.

Wood, L.J. (1972), Rural Marketing Pattern in Kenya, *Area*, Vol. 4. pp. 267-68.

Chapter 2

Ecological Framework of the Region

The ecological framework of a region is an indicator of the regional geographical individuality and is responsible for the present as well as future socio-economic development. Therefore, there is a need to explain the general ecological complex, i.e., physical environment, economic and socio-demographic organisations and their interrelated characteristics, which not only direct but determine the growth and development of all the economic activities including marketing.

The region under study, i.e., Central Hadaoti, is a sub-region of the Hadaoti Plateau---a distinct historico-geographical region of the Rajasthan State. The name 'Hadaoti' is derived from 'Hada' clan of the Rajputs who ruled over the erstwhile states of Kota and Bundi. The homogeneity and unity of historical, geographical, cultural, economic and social characteristics prevailing over the region and over a period of time endow it with a distinctiveness as compared to its adjoining areas. The geographical entity of the plateau can be recognised by the fact that this part of the country is virtually the northern extension of the Malwa Plateau and largely forms part of the 'Madhya Bharat Pathar'. The physiography, climate and soil characteristics of the region provide the area with a sort of physical homogeneity which can be seen in its human geography.

The Hadaoti Plateau forms a major region of the Rajasthan State, and includes the four districts of Bundi, Kota, Baran and Jhalawar. It can be divided into three sub-regions along diagonal lines, when adjusted with the district boundary. The Kota district has been identified as 'Central Hadaoti', which is a distinct geographical region of the Hadaoti Plateau. It is a riverian tract, well drained by river Chambal and its tributaries and located in the central part of the Hadaoti. The individuality of the region can be studied through its ecological framework, which need to be examined before any study of the region is to be attempted.

GEOGRAPHICAL ENVIRONMENT

Location

Central Hadaoti forms the central part of the Hadaoti Plateau comprising Kota district of Rajasthan, extending between 24°32′ to 25°53′N latitude and 75°36′ to 76°35′ E longitude having an area of 5,198 sq. kms. Administratively, its northern and north-eastern boundaries are along Bundi, Tonk and Sawai Madhopur districts, while the southern boundary borders the Jhalawar district. Along its south-eastern border is the Chittorgarh district and Madhya Pradesh State, and on its eastern boundary lies the Baran district and Madhya Pradesh State (Fig. 2.1)

Physiography: Geology and Relief

Geologically the region belongs to the Upper Vindhyan group of rocks. The stratographic succession of rocks exposed in this region is broadly as follows:

Recent: Alluvial soil (kankar)
Recent to sub-recent: Laterites and bauxite
Upper Cretaceous to Lower Eocene: Deccan trap
Palaeozoic: (a) Upper Vindhyan: Bhandar Series, Kaimur Series
(b) Lower Vindhyan: Samuri Series

Figure 2.1
Key Map of Central Hadaoti

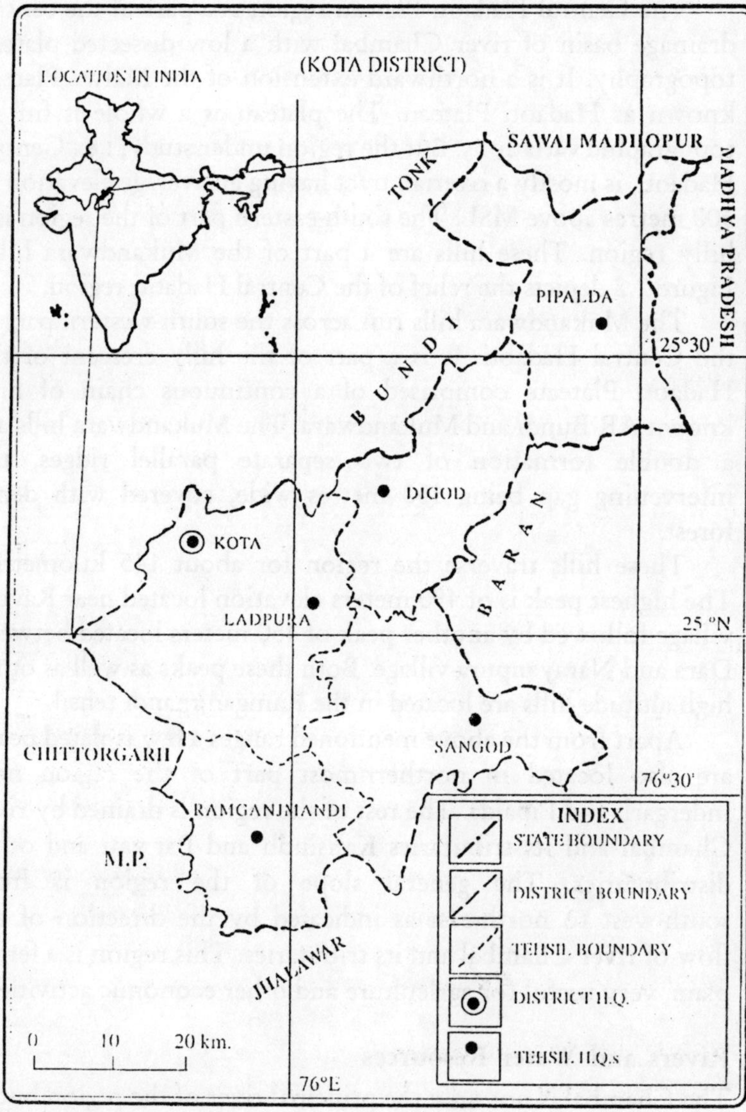

Structurally, the Vindhyan group of rocks are more or less stable---over a greater part of the area the eids are nearly horizontal but at places, they show steep deeps.

The Central Hadaoti Plateau region is a part of the central drainage basin of river Chambal with a low dissected plateau topography. It is a northward extension of the Malwa Plateau known as Hadaoti Plateau. The plateau as a whole is full of topographic variations. But the region under study, i.e., Central Hadaoti, is mostly a riverian tract having an average elevation of 300 metres above MSL. The south-eastern part of the region is a hilly region. These hills are a part of the Mukandwara hills. Figure 2.2 depicts the relief of the Central Hadaoti region.

The Mukandwara hills run across the south-western part of the Central Hadaoti. It is a part of the hilly crescent of the Hadaoti Plateau, comprised of a continuous chain of hills known AR Bundi and Mukandwara. The Mukandwara hills are a double formation of two separate parallel ridges, the intervening gap being 150 metres wide, covered with dense forest.

These hills traverse the region for about 145 kilometres. The highest peak is of 490 meters elevation located near Ravtha village followed by another peak of 450 meters located between Dara and Narayanpura village. Both these peaks as well as other high altitude hills are located in the Ramganjmandi tehsil.

Apart from the above mentioned ranges a few isolated peaks are also located in northernmost part of the region near Indergarh and Pipalda. The rest of the region is drained by river Chambal and its tributaries Kalisindh and Parwati and other distributaries. The general slope of the region is from south-west to north-east as indicated by the direction of the flow of river Chambal and its tributaries. This region is a fertile plain, very useful for agriculture and other economic activities.

Rivers and Water Resources

The Chambal is not only the principal river of the region but of the Rajasthan State. It is the only perennial river of the State. It

Figure 2.2
Central Hadaoti: Relief and Drainage

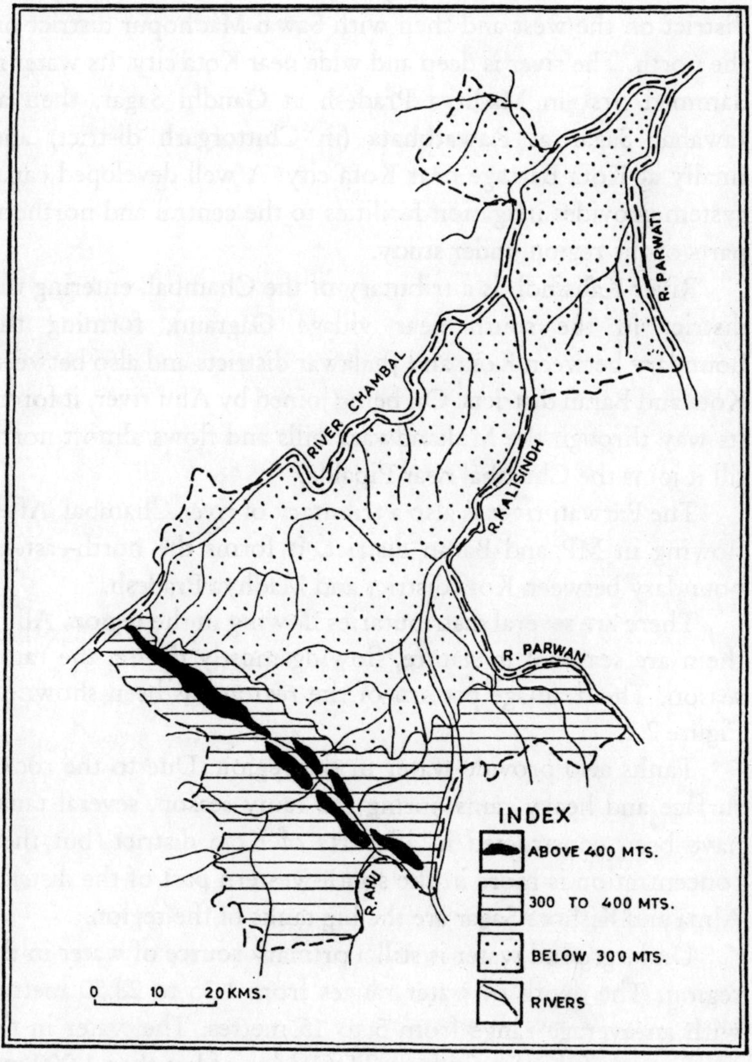

takes its origin in Madhya Pradesh near Mahu and enters the Kota district on the west at the trijunction of the boundaries of Kota, Bundi and Chittorgarh districts and, for a greater part of its course, forms the boundary of Kota district first with Bundi district on the west and then with Sawai Madhopur district on the north. The river is deep and wide near Kota city. Its water is dammed first in Madhya Pradesh at Gandhi Sagar, then at Jawahar Sagar at Rawatbhata (in Chittorgarh district) and finally at Kota Barrage near Kota city. A well developed canal system provides irrigation facilities to the central and northern parts of the region under study.

River Kalisindh is a tributary of the Chambal, entering the district in the south near village Gagraun, forming the boundary between Kota and Jhalawar districts and also between Kota and Baran districts. On being joined by Ahu river, it forces its way through the Mukandwara hills and flows almost north till it joins the Chambal near Pipalda.

The Parwati river is also a tributary of river Chambal. After flowing in MP and Baran district, it forms the north-eastern boundary between Kota district and Madhya Pradesh.

There are several distributaries flowing in the region. All of them are seasonal in nature, flowing mostly during the rainy season. The drainage pattern of the region has been shown in Figure 2.2.

Tanks also provide water in the region. Due to the rocky surface and heavy rains during the rainy season, several tanks have been constructed in all parts of Kota district, but their concentration is more in the south-western part of the district. Alma and Kishore Sagar are the big tanks of the region.

Underground water is still a primary source of water in the region. The depth of water ranges from 1.35 to 28.50 metres, with an average range from 5 to 15 metres. The water in the major part of the district have TDC value of less than 1,000 mg. per litre which is suitable both for irrigation and domestic purposes. The hydrogeological survey revealed that the central and north-western parts of the district have high potentiality for ground water.

Climate

Though latitudinally situated in the sub-tropical region, the climate of the Central Hadaoti is characteristically 'monsoon' as that of the rest of India, and as such the year is markedly divided into seasons. All the elements of climate, i.e., temperature, pressure, wind, rainfall and relative humidity show well marked seasonal variations (Fig. 2.3). Thus, November to February is the winter season but marked change in temperature and pressure is not felt earlier than March, when it gradually begins to get warmer. By the middle of June it is extremely sultry and the expected rains usually break with dramatic suddenness often in the last week of June. Thenceforth, till the middle of September the rainy season continues followed by fall in temperatures to welcome winter. The three well marked seasons are:

The Winter Season: The rains are almost over by the second week of September though sometimes a few delayed showers are not uncommon. There is a gradual decrease in temperature from 29.6° in September to 16.6°C in January. The sky remains cloudless and perfectly blue, temperature and humidity also greatly decline. January is the coldest month with the mean daily minimum temperatures at 10.6°C and the mean maximum 24.3°C. A casual visit of a cold air mass may bring down the temperatures, bringing in a cold waves which may at time last for a few days. The season is usually dry with light winds, though a casual rainfall may occur from a travelling shallow depression from the west or north-west. Such rainfall is locally known as '*mahavat*' which although very small in amount is of great utility for the 'rabi' crops. On an average, winter rains amount to about 4.2 cms. which may be 2.5 per cent of the total annual rainfall.

Figure 2.3
Annual Rainfall and Mean Monthly Temperature at Kota

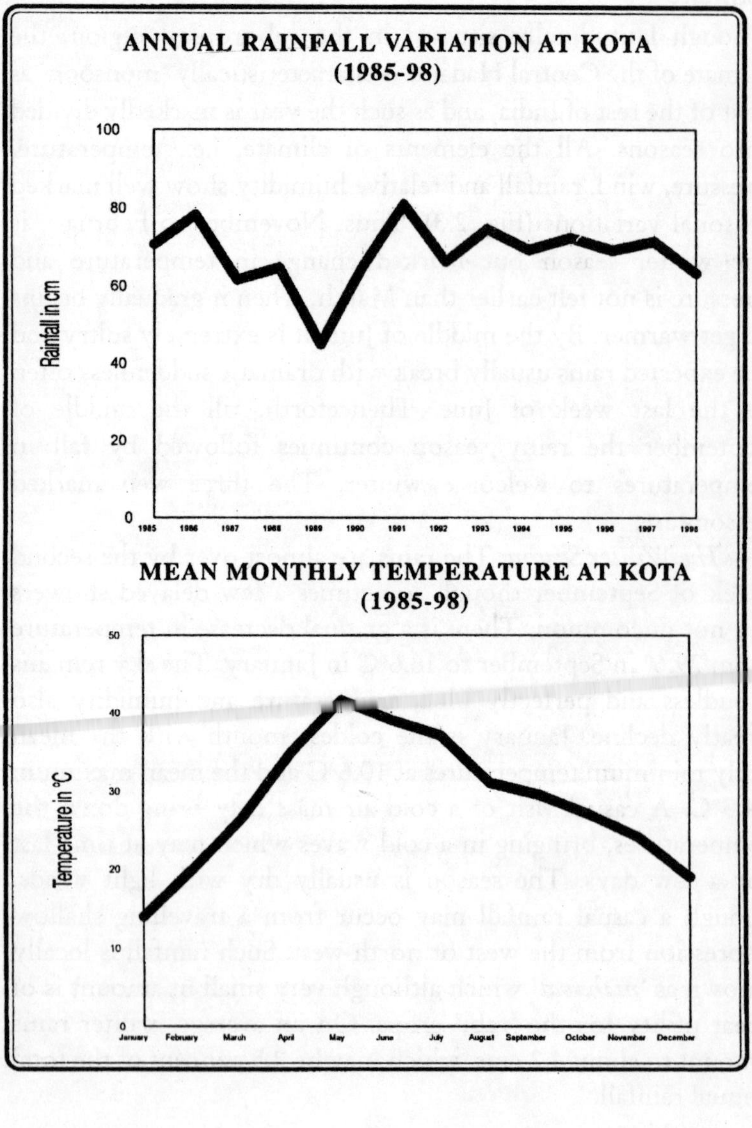

The Summer Season: From early March to the middle of June the season is truly hot. High temperatures with wafts of suffocating duststorms known as '*aandhi*', intolerable hot air during the day known as '*loo*' and variable winds are some of the common characteristics. Both day and night temperatures increase rapidly and in May (the hottest month), the mean daily maximum temperature is 42.6°C, while the mean minimum is 29.7°C. The highest temperature reached at Kota was 47.8°C. The normal velocity of wind is 12.5 km. per hour with the air still dry and sky almost clear and the relative humidity reaches its maximum of 75 per cent.

The Rainy Season: The change from hot to wet season is generally sudden when the monsoon is said to 'burst'. The region is in the grip of monsoon usually by 25th of June. On some fine day an intensive storm with thunder, lightning and rain occurs with dramatic suddenness. July and August are the wettest months in which 75 per cent of the annual rainfall occurs, another 25 per cent being accounted for in June and September. The average annual rainfall of the region is 88.25 cm. The heaviest rainfall was recorded at Chechat on 29th June, 1945, when 38.33 cms rainfall occurred in 24 hours. On an average there are 40 rainy days (days with rain of 2.5 mm or more in a year). The distributional pattern within the region varies from southern to north-eastern part.

In general, the climate of the region under study is healthy, but malarious during the rainy season. The impact of the climate is apparent on all the economic activities, including marketing.

Natural Vegetation

The forest cover of the Central Hadaoti is of 1,16,426 hectares which is 22.34 per cent of the total area of the region. The main concentration of forest is in the south-western parts, mainly on the Mukandwara hills. The forests of the region under study fall under Northern Tropical Dry Deciduous Forest with the following sub-types:

(i) *Anogeissus Pendula Forest*: Main species found in the region are *dhakra, gurjan, bel, tendu*, etc.
(ii) *Miscellaneous Forest*: Main species of *khejra, khair, kalam, amaltas, kohra, bahera, gurjan*, etc.
(iii) *Babul (Acacia arabica wild) Forest*: *Babul* mixed with khejra is the representative flora found in these forests.

Other species of trees found in the forests of the region include *dhau, bahera, mahuwa, salar, chhola, shisham, gular, jamun, neem, pipal, aam, semal*, etc. The grasses commonly found are *laplu, polard, ratarda, surwal, karar, bhalk* and *chlona*. There are many '*birs*' in Morak and Kanwas ranges.

The major forest produce of the region consists of timber, firewood and charcoal. The minor forest produce consists of *katha*, gum, *tendu* leaves, honey, wax and grasses. *Tendu* leaves are collected for manufacture of *biris*, while *katha* is extracted from the *Acacia catechu* tree. Some flowers and fruits are also collected and used as edibles.

Soils

The dominant type of soil in the Central Hadaoti region is alluvial. These soils have been brought down by rivers like Chambal, Kalisindh, Parwati and their tributaries. Since this region is a northern extension of the Malwa Plateau, black soil is found in its southern parts, while reddish brown soil is the dominant type of soil in Ladpura, Sultanpur and Itawa tehsils. According to the new comprehensive system of soil classification, the soils of this region are in Chromusterts category. These soils are suitable for cultivation of various types of crops.

POPULATION

Ecologically, population is a group of individuals of any kind of organism, but in the present context population means human population. They have psycho-biological structures and have birth, growth, dispersion, sex ratio and death. So the study of population involves a study of fertility, mortality, age and sex ratio, occupational structure, urbanisation, and settlement and their spatio-temporal variations. These elements are called demographic components and have direct impact on the ecosystem of a region. The complex environment-population interrelationships not only direct but determine the eco-balance of a region, in other words, they provide a base for sustainable development. Therefore, a brief analysis of the demographic structure of the region under study is necessary.

In the 1991 census, separate population data for the present Kota district are not available because till 1991 Baran district was a part of Kota. All the data related to Kota district have been compiled on the basis of tehsil-wise data. For the present analysis data have been obtained based on the 1991 census publication *The Population of Rajasthan* by B.K. Pitaliya and other census publications. The total population of Kota district (Central Hadaoti) was 12,20,505. As in case of other districts the region has also registered a steady growth of population and during 1981-91 the growth rate was 32.20 per cent. The pattern of decennial growth of population cannot be traced out because of the division of this district into two—Kota and Baran—but the combined trend shows a steady growth of population except during the 1911-21 decade when the population decreased due to large scale famine not only in the region but in whole state.

Distribution and Density: The population distribution in this region has little variation except in regions adjoining Kota city. Because of the presence of Kota city, Ladpura tehsil has four to five times more population in comparison with other tehsils of the region. The following table indicates the tehsil-wise population and density of population in Central Hadaoti:

Figure 2.4
Central Hadaoti: Distribution of Population, 1991

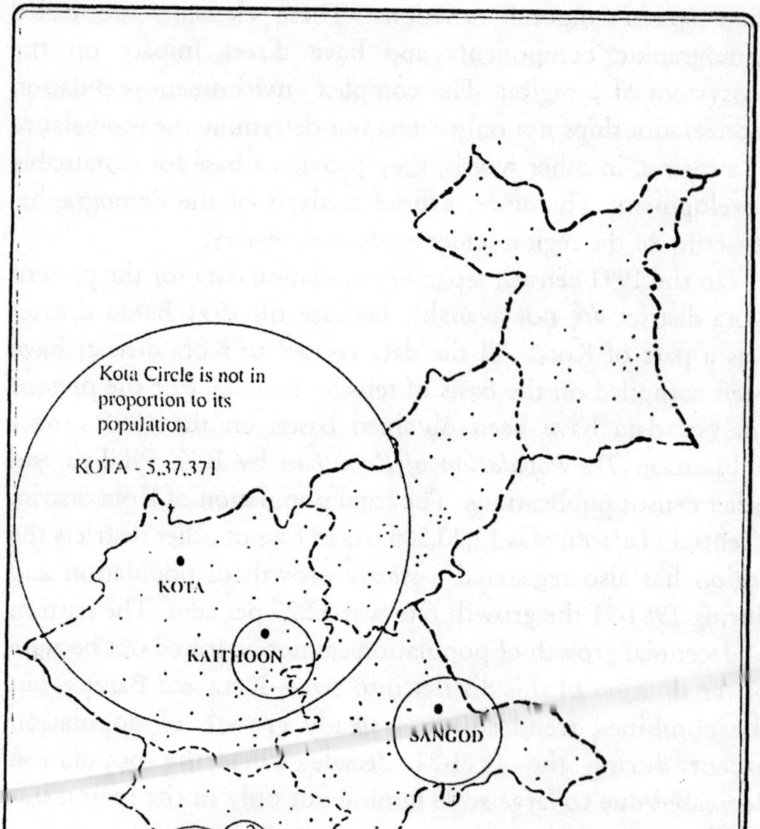

Table 2.1
Tehsil-wise Density of Population, 1991

	Tehsil	*Male*	*Female*	*Total*	*Density per sq. km*
1.	Pipalda	67286	59834	127120	143
2.	Digod	65430	58394	123824	136
3.	Ladpura	354280	308733	663013	429
4.	Ramganjmandi	89369	78991	168188	
5.	Sangod	72507	65681	138188	130
	Total	648872	571633	12,20,505	235

It becomes clear from the above table that Ladpura tehsil has the maximum population with 6,63,013 persons followed by Ramganjmandi with 1,68,360 persons, while Pipalda tehsil has 1,27,120 persons. The general distribution pattern has been shown in Fig. 2.4. The highest density of 429 persons per sq.km. is seen in Ladpura tehsil, followed by Ramganjmandi with 212, Pipalda 143, Digod 136 and Sangod tehsil 130 only. The average density of population of the region is 235 persons per sq.km. (Fig. 2.5).

Sex Ratio: In the region under study, there are 881 females per thousand males. This ratio is 893 in rural areas and 852 in urban areas. In Sangod tehsil there are 905 females per thousand males, which is the highest in the region; while in Ladpura tehsil it is lowest with 871 females per thousand males. The number of females per thousand males is 889, 892 and 884 in Pipalda, Digod and Ramganjmandi tehsils respectively.

Occupational Structure: According to the 1991 census, 65.95 per cent population of the Kota district is in the category of non-workers. The percentage of industrial category of main workers was 30.30, which includes nine categories, viz., cultivators, agricultural labourers, livestock and forestry, mining and quarrying, manufacturing constructions, trade and commerce, transport, and other services. Among these

Figure 2.5

Central Hadaoti: Sex Ratio and Density of Population, 1991

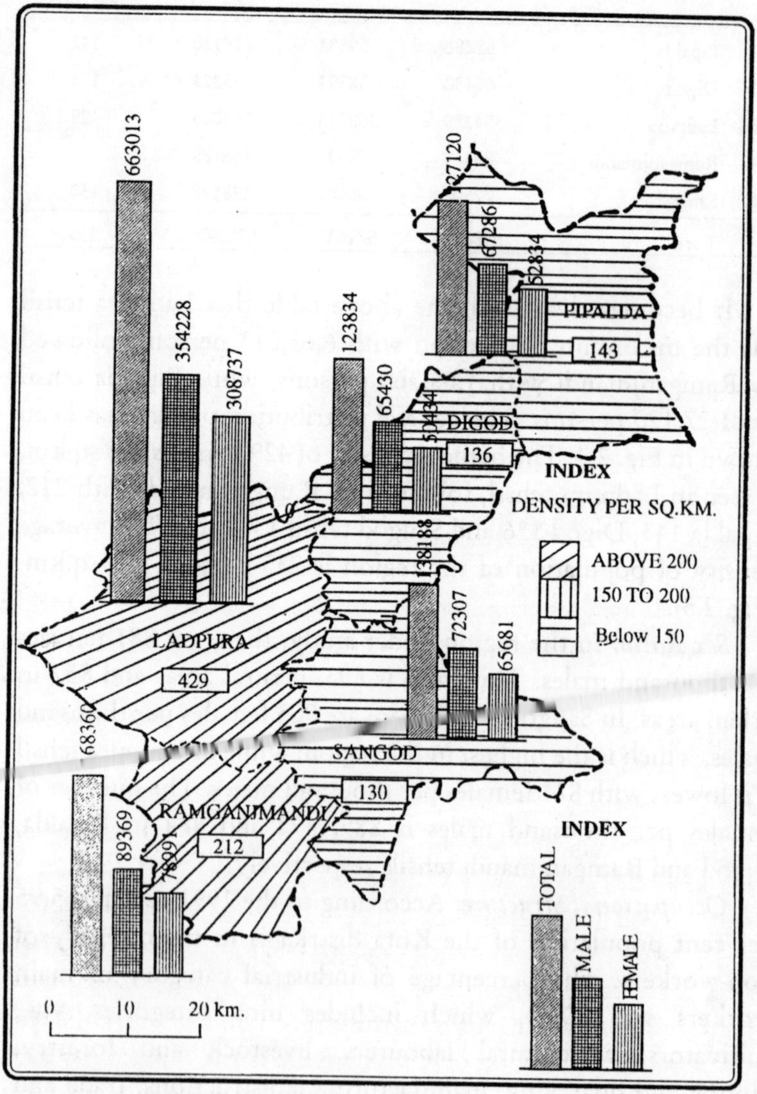

percentage of cultivators is highest, i.e., 8.63 per cent. The following table indicates the overall occupational structure of the region:

Table 2.2

Occupational Structure of Central Hadaoti, 1991

Category	*Population*	*Percentage of Total*
Industrial Category	369852	30.30
Main workers		
(i) Cultivators	105313	8.63
(ii) Agricultural labourers	47796	3.91
(iii) Livestock, forestry, etc.	8872	0.72
(iv) Mining and quarrying	20124	1.65
(v) (a) Manufacturing, processing service and repair in household industry	4607	0.37
(b) Manufacturing, other than household industry	44973	3.68
(vi) Construction	17166	1.40
(vii) Trade and commerce	41499	3.40
(viii) Transport, storage and communications	18058	1.48
(ix) Other services	61444	5.03
(x) Marginal workers	45658	3.74
(xi) Non-workers	804995	65.95

Rural-Urban Population: It is interesting to note that the region under study shows a balance between rural and urban population. The percentage of rural population in 1991 was 49.47, while 50.53 per cent population was recorded as urban. The total rural population of the region, i.e., 6,03,745 is inhabited in 811 villages. On the other hand, there are seven towns in the region, among which Kota is the biggest having a population of 5,37,371 in 1991. The following table indicates the urban population of the region:

Table 2.3

Urban Population (1991) of Central Hadaoti

	Urban Centre	Category	Population
1.	Kota	M.C.	537371
2.	Kaithoon	M	16040
3.	Udaipura	CT	6071
4.	Ramganjmandi	M	20875
5.	Satalkheri	CT	9742
6.	Suket	CT	11056
7.	Sangod	M	15603

M.C. -Municipal Council, M-Municipality, CT-Census Town.

Scheduled Caste and Scheduled Tribe Population: The percentage of SC and ST population in the region under study is 20.27 and 9.10 respectively in 1991. The following table indicates the tehsil-wise SC/ST population of the region:

Table 2.4

Tehsil-wise SC/ST Population, 1991

	Tehsil	SC Population	ST population
1.	Pipalda	32,399	28,572
2.	Digod	30,466	[illegible]
3.	Ladpura	1,10,613	34,230
4	Ramganjmandi	44,147	18,820
5.	Sangod	29,804	13,575
	Total	2,47,429	1,17,142

Literacy: The total number of literates in the region was 5,42,929 (in 1991) which was 44.48 per cent of the total population. The literacy among males is higher at 30.38 per cent than 14.10 per cent for females. Ramganjmandi tehsil was having 57,657 literate persons followed by 40,625 in Digod tehsil. Recently, the literacy rate has increased due to the intensive literacy drive programme and in the next census it will be much higher.

ECONOMIC AND SOCIAL ORGANISATION

The third aspect of ecological framework is the economic and social organisation, which is the result of man-environment interaction. The entire development system, i.e., economic, social, cultural and even political is an integral part of any ecosystem. The growth and development of civilisation is nothing but man's use of the earth's surface and/or environment. In order to fulfill their demands, human beings always use nature and its resources and develop economic and social organisations. The success of the organisations depends upon their adjustment with the ecosystem. The concept of sustainable development has also been evolved for co-ordination between man's activities of development and natural environment. A brief description of economic organisation—agriculture, livestock, mining, manufacturing, transport and marketing—as well as of social organisation is necessary for an analysis of the marketing system.

Economic Organisation

Land Use Pattern

The land use pattern of the Central Hadaoti region is given in the following Table 2.5 and has been depicted in Fig. 2.6-A.

It becomes clear from the table that the net sown area is 51.52 per cent which indicates the dominance of agriculture in the region. The area sown more than once is 23.19 per cent, thus total cropped area of the region is 74.73 per cent. The forests are spread in 118,722 hectares, which amounts to 22.78 per cent of the total area. The percentage of area not available for cultivation is 12.94, while fallow land is of 5.06 per cent.

Figure 2.6
Central Hadaoti: (a) Land Utilisation, 1996-97;
(b) Production of Important Crops, 1996-97

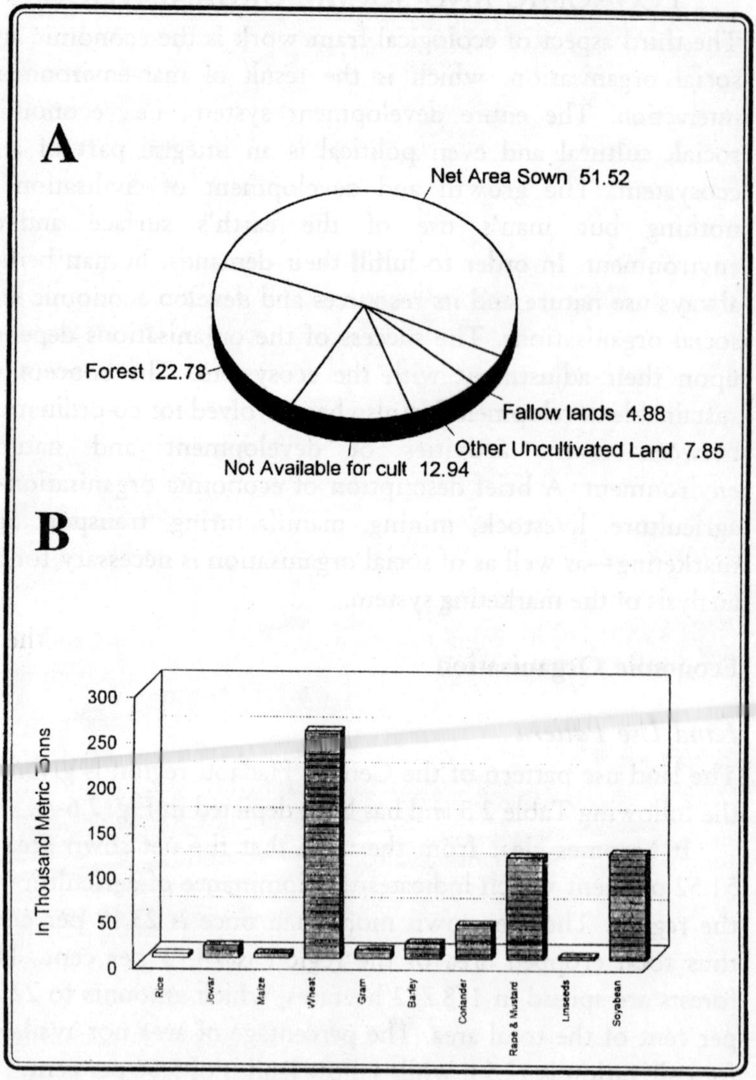

Table 2.5

Land Utilisation of the Central Hadaoti Plateau (Kota District), 1996-97

Land use categories	*Area*	*Percentage of total*
1. Forest	1,18,722	22.78
2. Not available for cultivation	67,472	12.94
(i) Area under non-agricultural uses	27,361	5.27
(ii) Barren and unculturable land	40,111	7.69
3. Other uncultivated land	40,951	7.85
(i) Permanent pastures and other grazing land	13,863	2.66
(ii) Land under misc. tree crops and groves	718	0.14
(iii) Land excluding fallow lands cultural waste land	26,370	5.06
4. Fallow lands	25,436	4.88
(i) Fallow lands other than current fallow	16,151	3.09
(ii) Current fallow	9,285	1.78
5. Net sown area	2,68,502	51.52
6. Total cropped area	3,89,397	74.73
7. Area sown more than once	1,20,895	23.19

Source: Agricultural Statistics Rajasthan, 1996-97, pp. 304. Directorate of Economics and Statistics, Rajasthan, Jaipur.

Principal Crops: There are two main crop seasons in the district, *kharif* and *rabi.* The chief *kharif* or rainfed crops include jowar, maize, rice, moong and groundnut, while in the *rabi* season wheat, barley, gram, coriander, soyabean, etc., are grown. Among other crops sugarcane, *dehinia*, rape and mustard, linseed as well as fruits and vegetables are also grown. A small quantity of land is also used for opium production under government licence---its production is purchased by the concerned department. The following Table 2.6 indicates the area and production of important crops in the region under study.

It becomes clear from the table that wheat is the most important food crop of the region, sown in 91,249 hectares and its production was 2,52,336 MT in 1996-97. Jowar, maize, barley and rice are other food crops. The production of rape and mustard was 1,13,187 MT in 1996-97. This region is also an important producer of soyabean. Gram, linseed and coriander are among other important crops of the region. Fig.2.6-B shows the production of important crops in the Central Hadaoti region.

Table 2.6

Area and Production of Important Crops in Central Hadaoti, 1996-97

Crops	*Area*	*Production*
1. Rice	2931	4423
2. Jowar	18159	14043
3. Maize	7223	5115
4. Wheat	91249	252336
5. Gram	10546	9733
6. Barley	1270	17076
7. Coriander	33962	37712
8. Rape and Mustard	91289	113187
9. Linseed	6436	3536
10. Soyabean	97257	117701

Source: Agricultural Statistics, Rajasthan, 1996-97, Directorate of Economics and Statistics, Rajasthan, Jaipur.

Irrigation: The region under study is endowed with good irrigation facilities. River Chambal is the main source of water. The construction of Kota Barrage near Kota city was completed in year 1954. The Kota Barrage has been constructed to provide irrigation facilities through a well developed canal system having a length of 425 km. of main canal and 560 km. of distributaries spread over Kota, Bundi, Baran, Tonk and Sawai Madhopur districts of Rajasthan as well as in parts of Madhya Pradesh. As much as 1,35,501 hectares of land in Kota district is irrigated by the Chambal canal system. The following table indicates the total irrigated area by various sources:

Table 2.7
Area Irrigated by Different Sources in Central Hadaoti

	Total Irrigated Area (in hectare)
1. Canals	1,49,625
(i) Chambal System	1,35,501
(ii) Others	14,044
2. Tanks	708
3. Tubewells	35,879
4. Other wells	50,740
5. Other sources	8,303
Total	2,45,254

Source: Agricultural Statistics, Rajasthan, 1996-97, Directorate of Economics and Statistics, Jaipur.

Livestock: The Central Hadaoti region is an agricultural region and livestock always supports agricultural activity and also provides livelihood both subsistence and commercial to a section of population. Table 2.8 indicates the number of livestock in the Kota district.

Table 2.8
Livestock in Central Hadaoti

Type	*Total Number*	*Type*	*Total Number*
1. Cattle	4,94,983	5. Horses and Ponies	650
2. Buffaloes	1,42,994	6. Mules	241
3. Sheep	30,994	7. Donkeys	1628
4. Goats	1,85,754	8. Pigs	16,735
		9. Camels	2,633
Total			6,66,707

Sources Based on 15th Census of Livestock, Rajasthan, 1992, Statistical Abstract, Rajasthan, 1994.

Minerals: Building stone constitutes the main mineral wealth of the region. Central Hadaoti is the second largest producer of building stones in Rajasthan, after Jodhpur district.

Sandstone is available all over the district, but more prominently in Ladpura tehsil. In western part of the district Rath Kankara, Borabas, Nanta, Kasar, Rautha, Balwan are important centres of sandstone mining.

Limestone is quarried from the Vindhan System of formation in Ramganjmandi, Mork, Suket, Dara, Kasar, Chechat and Pipalda areas. The stone is used for flooring and is popularly known as 'Kota stone'. Kota stone is in great demand not only in the country but also in west Asia. The mining of other building materials such as masonry stone, bajari sand and lime is also done in this region. Small deposits of red clay, glass sand, dolomite and kankar are also found. Occurrence of iron ore, fine clay, red and yellow ochre have also been reported but their mining is commercially not viable.

Manufacturing: Although Central Hadaoti is agriculturally important region its industrial base is also strong. The rapid industrial development at Kota city has placed this region on the industrial map not only of the state but in India. Prior to the sixties, this region was backward in respect of industries and only small scale and cottage industries were in existence. Production and abundant availability of electric power from the Gandhi Sagar and Rana Pratap Sagar on the Chambal river and later from the atomic reactor of Rawat Bhata have revolutionised the opportunities of large scale industries in the region particularly in the environs of Kota city. Besides the availability of industrial power, the availability and utilisation of perennial water supply from river Chambal, the midway location on the Delhi-Bombay broad gauge railway, abundant supply of local labour, and the opportunities of market are the factors which favour industrial activities in this region.

The main industries which have developed in and around Kota city are chemical, engineering, textile, metal, plastic, plyboard and rubber goods. There are eight chemical factories producing caustic soda, PVC, soda-ash, sodium silicate, zinc oxide, fertilisers and other chemicals. There are 13

Figure 2.7

Central Hadaoti: Transportation Network

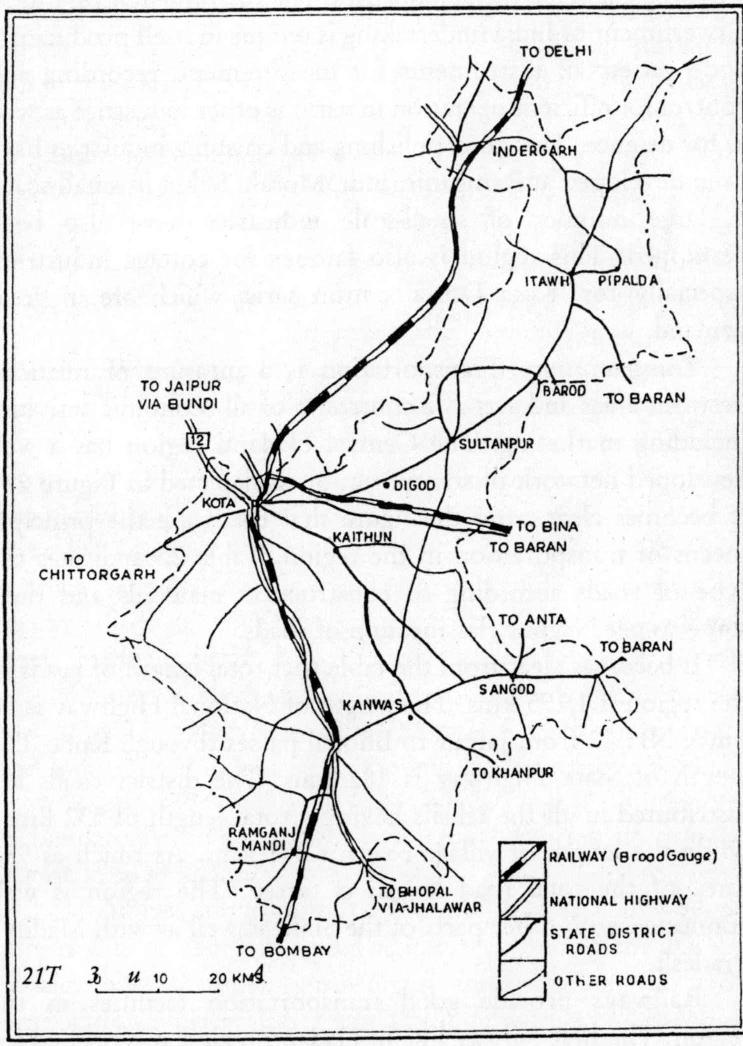

establishments manufacturing cables, precision instruments, aluminium conductors, radio-components and tractor parts. There are five textile mills weaving rayons, nylon thread and wool tops, and ten metal industries. The Instrumentation Ltd., a Government of India undertaking is unique in itself producing a wide variety of instruments for measurement, recording and control for efficient operation in various other industries as well as for defence. The stone polishing and crushing industries have been developed at Ramganjmandi, Morak, Suket in small scale. A large number of small-scale industries have also been developed. This region is also famous for cottage industries, especially for 'Kota Doria' cotton saris, which are in great demand.

Transportation: Transportation is a measure of relations between areas and acts as a controller of all economic activities including marketing. The Central Hadaoti region has a well developed network of transportation as depicted in Figure 2.7. It becomes clear from the figure that roads are the principal means of transportation in the region. Table 2.9 indicates the type of roads according to construction materials and their status as per Nagpur classification of roads.

It becomes clear from the table that total length of roads in the region is 1,195 kms. The length of National Highway is 90 kms.; NH 12 from Jaipur to Bhopal passes through Kota. The length of State Highway is 182 kms. The district roads are distributed in all the tehsils having a total length of 532 kms., while the length of village roads is 391 kms. As much as 988 kms. of the total road length is tarred. The region is well connected with other parts of the State as well as with Madhya Pradesh.

Railways provide good transportation facilities in the region. The first railway line in Hadaoti region was opened for traffic from Guna (in Madhya Pradesh) to Baran in erstwhile Kota state in May 1899. It became useful only in 1906 when it was extended up to Kota. Another railway line, Nagda to Mathura via Kota was opened for traffic in 1908. This broad gauge line is of great significance because it connects Delhi with Bombay. Another addition of railway in this region is Kota to Chittorgarh railway line. All the railways in this region are broad gauge. Kota is now an important railway junction. The other railway stations in the region are Ramganjmandi, Morak, Gopal Road, Kamalpura, Darah, Raotha Road, Dhani Kasar, Dadh Devi, Alnia, Dakaniay Talab, Digod and Indergarh.

Table 2.9

Types of Roads, 1996

		Length in kilometres
(a)	*Categories*	
	1. Painted (B.T.)	988
	2. Metalled (W.B.M.)	63
	3. Gravelled (G.R.)	130
	4. Fair Weather (F.R.)	14
	Total	1195
(b)	*Status of Roads*	
	1. National Highway	90
	2. State Highway	182
	3. Main District Roads	221
	4. Other District Roads	311
	5. Village Roads	391
	Total	1195

Kota also has an airport but so far it has not been used for regular air service. Only after 1991 casual air service was started between Delhi and Kota via Jaipur.

Social Organisation

The social organisation of a region is the outcome of the long play of factors---historical as well as geo-economic. The present social system of the region has been developed over various historical phases.

In the early phase of human settlement, traces of prehistoric man have been found in central Bundi range and along the banks of river Chambal and its tributaries. It seems that during the fourth interglacial period, there was continuous human settlement. Mention of river Chambal (Charmanavati) is found in the Puranic text (*Gazetteer*, Kota). The early history of the region is shrounded in the darkness of time and little is known about it, but for the fact that the Malav people, who were uprooted during the invasion of Alexander the Great in 327 BC, came and settled down in the northern part of Malwa (Hadaoti region) (Tripathi, 1960: 244). On the basis of several specimens of old copper coins and a few pieces of silver found in the region, Cunninghan has determined the age of colonisation of this region as being between 500 and 100 BC (Cunningham, 1871: 264). This part of the country was the stronghold of the Jains.

The history of the settlement of this part of the country during medieval times is more or less the story of the friendly or unfriendly relations of Hada Rajputs with the central authority and later on with the British rulers. In the latter period of the nineteen century, perhaps in 1872, a new principality of Jhalawar came into being as a separate State. The subsequent history of Kota upto independence in 1947 was simply a description of the struggle among the royal chiefs of the three States of Hadaoti and the Britishers. The social life of this region was similar to that of the other parts of the Rajasthan State.

The social groups are still divided mainly by caste and religion. The old caste-ridden social hierarchy has now been changed but there is still a tendency to form social groups based on caste. These social groups not only perform social functions but are also active in local politics. The main castes of the region are Brahmins, Rajputs, Mahajans, Kayasthas and also occupational castes like Khati (carpenter), Lohar (blacksmiths), Sunar (goldsmiths), Dhobis (washerman), Darzis (tailors), Kumars (earthen pot maker), Mali (gardeners), etc. The agricultural castes are Jat, Dhakar, Gujar and Meena. The Muslims also form a large section of society. The schedule caste and schedule tribes also have their social groups.

The Hindu and Muslim are two important religious groups. Other religious groups include Jains, Sikhs, Christians and Buddhists. In terms of language, the region has its own regional dialect known as *Hadoti*, which is considered as a branch of Rajasthani. The festivals, fairs and rituals play a vital role in social life. The impact of social structure can also be seen on economic activities. After independence rapid social changes have occurred due to the spread of education, increased transport and communication facilities, economic development, government incentives and also due to increased awareness about rights and laws.

The ecological framework described in this chapter provides a base for regional economic development, including the development of marketing system. At the same time it also helps in planning for the sustainable development.

References

Cunningham, A. (1871), *Archaeological Survey of India*, Vol. II, p. 264.

Gupta, S. (1982), Rajasthan District Gazetteers, Kota, (1960), *History of Ancient India*, p. 244.

Source of Data

Agricultural Statistics—Rajasthan, 1996-97, Directorate of Economics and Statistics, Rajasthan, Jaipur.

Statistical Abstract, Rajasthan—1994, Directorate of Economics and Statistics, Jaipur.

Director Census Operations Rajasthan, Jaipur.

Zila Sanskaiya Ruprekha---Kota, 1994, Directorate of Economics and Statistics, Jaipur.

The Population of Rajasthan, B.K. Pitaliya, 1997, Kishore Book Depot, Jaipur.

Population Projection (1991-2011) Rajasthan, Directorate of Economics and Statistics, Rajasthan, Jaipur.

Chapter 3

Growth of Markets and the Ecological Complex

The growth and development of marketing and markets, or market-place exchange system is the result of a long play of factors, both geo-economic as well as socio-cultural and historical. The history of the development of marketing and trade is closely associated with the history of civilisation. Simple, unorganised and rudimentary trade or exchange of commodities is as old as man's society. When man's orbit of activities was narrow, he used to apply the simple exchange or barter system. With the growing complexity in life and society, the pattern of trade and marketing system has also become complex. The regional ecological framework plays a vital role not only in growth of markets and marketing but is also responsible for spatial linkages both inter and intra-markets. Therefore, there is a need to explain the growth of marketing and to examine the rôle of ecological factors which direct and determine the existing regional pattern of marketing.

Growth of Marketing and Markets

Early man believed in self-sufficiency and had no idea either of exchange or trade. His very limited wants were satisfied either by his immediate environment or by the place he used to move in search of food, water, favourable climate, etc. His nomadic culture too had some sort of free exchange of petty articles in the form of gifts or reciprocal exchange of needed items. When man started living in groups, whatever their size, he began an exchange of commodities. The regional variations in geographical environment, resource availability and man's skill to utilise them were some of the fundamental causes responsible for the development of trade. "Accidental surpluses, specialisation of production, presence of a rare and desirable item, or the need for essential products, gave rise to the exchange of goods which, in turn made man enlarge his knowledge of goods and his desire to obtain them" (Mulvihill and Mulvihill, 1970: 9).

The earliest system of marketing was no doubt barter, i.e., exchange of commodities. Its first form was silent barter, in which one left his product at some selected place, while the person who required that article also left his product and waited for some time. If the first person took away the offering, it meant the offer had been accepted. Later on, barter system become common and was in practice even after the development of coins as the medium of exchange. This system is still prevalent in many parts of India including the region under study, as observed by Berry (1967: 89), "there are still simple cultures in which exchange takes the form of reciprocal gift giving or the redistribution of goods, and barter is the rule".

With the development of agriculture and with improvement in living conditions, man soon realised the advantage of trade and he began to produce more than what was required to meet local needs. This kind of trade too was limited to certain favourable geographical locations. The most important aspect of the development of market-place trade was the beginning of periodic markets. These periodic markets have been developed all over the world to fulfill the limited wants of the people and also to dispose of the limited surplus available for sale after satisfying their own needs. Periodic markets are of two types: (i) weekly or bi-weekly or on some specific day of the month, and (ii) fairs. The difference between the first type of markets and the other lies in the fact that the former is primarily an assemblage of traders on some specific days of the week or fortnight to facilitate retail operations, while a fair may be held once or twice in a year and become the focal point for the economic, religious and cultural activities. Cleef (1937: 39) has observed that "fairs rank among the oldest as well as the most fascinating of trading institutions".

Only a few geographical studies have been done regarding the origin of market-places, that even these are still very tentative (Hodder and Lee, 1974: 137). The orthodox theory starts from individual self-sufficiency to barter, followed by periodic assembly of buyers and sellers and finally the establishment of permanent shops and markets as well as the start of daily and long-distance trading. Some others believe that market centres are the result of long-distance trading in order to fulfil the demands of a region. This has been explained by Hodder (1974: 137) as a hypothesis, that markets are the end product of long-distance trading and contacts, together with the conditioning factors of the kind of physical security that can ensure the market-place and a sufficiently high population density to make regular face-to-face contacts of people practicable. Similar views have been explained by Polanyi (1957), Pirenne (1936), Berry (1967) and others. In fact, there are some common characteristics and/or sequences of market development throughout the world with regional differences. Following Hodder and Lee (1974), a modified model of sequential development of markets has been depicted in Fig. 3.1 (A & B), which is also applicable for the region under study. Figure 3.1 A shows the shift from mobile traders to establishment of periodic markets (P) to daily marketing (D); while Figure 3.1 B indicates a direct development process, i.e., mobile merchants to daily marketing.

Figure 3.1
Sequential Development of Markets

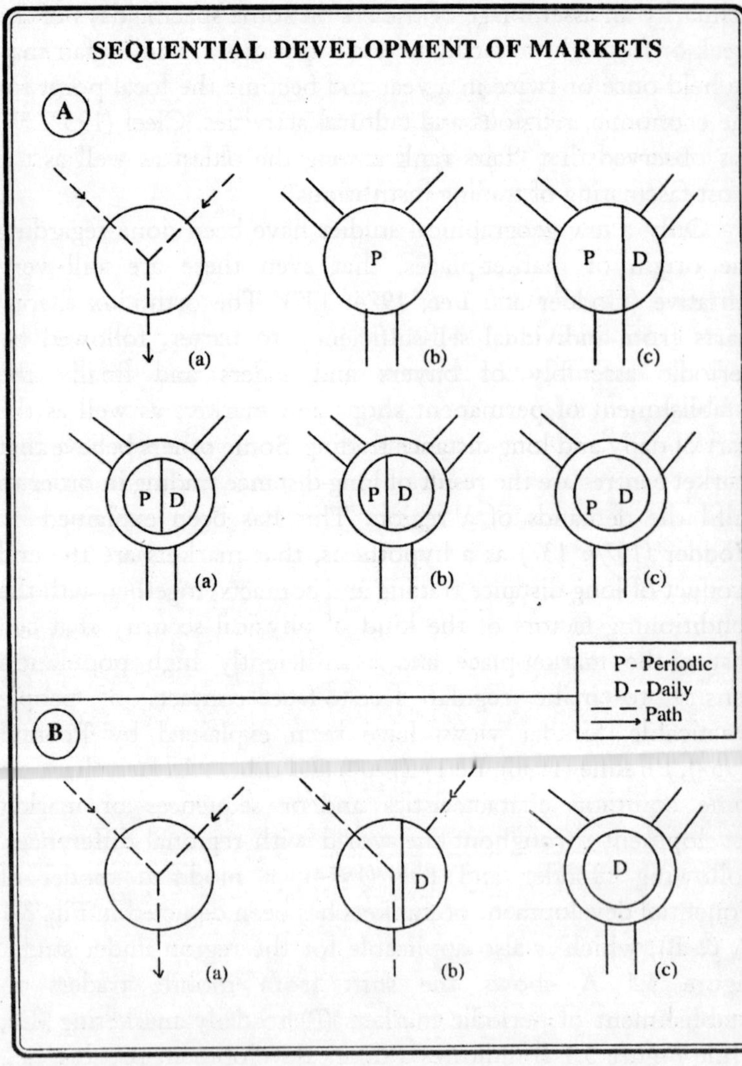

Growth of Market System in Central Hadaoti

Due to the absence of historical records concerning trade and commerce, no attempt has been made to trace the development of marketing system in the Rajasthan in general and Hadaoti region in particular. The present analysis is based on scattered historical references and a preliminary attempt to trace the important characteristics of marketing activity during ancient, medieval and modern periods.

Ancient Period

In primitive cultures, when man was a nomad and used to meet his needs by hunting or making use of forest products, there was no question of any reciprocal exchange. The various economic systems (including exchange and/or marketing) have their beginning with the development of a social institution. In fact, "the exchange system is merely one aspect of regularities of social relationships" (Belshaw, 1965: 7). During the ancient period, northern India already had a developed marketing system as well as market centres. But there is no reference of any important commercial mart in the Hadaoti region. Only a few archaeological sites testify to the antiquity of the region. It is likely that in early times the tract might have been occupied by Malavas because they appear to have settled around Karkotnagar about 45 miles (72 kms.) north-west of Kota (Chattopadhyaya, 1958: 149). The Allahabad Pillar Inscription mentions that Samudra Gupta uprooted Acyuta Nagasena, a king of the Kota family in the course of his campaign in north India (Tripathi, 1969: 288) Later, the region had been ruled by the Maurya dynasty and afterwards passed into the hands of Paramaras and later on Bhils and Minas had established their hold in the region (Majumdar, 1957: 69).

During this period most of the population was scattered in the form of groups of a few families or in very small villages. The villages were self-sufficient, or in other words, their demands were very limited. Their primary necessities were food and clothing, which were fulfilled within the village itself or by reciprocal exchange. The non-existence of markets during ancient period in the region was due to:

(i) small and scattered population,
(ii) very limited demand,
(iii) harsh environmental conditions,
(iv) lack of transport facilities,
(v) danger of dacoity and robbery, and
(v) overall economic backwardness.

Medieval Period

During the medieval period this region was administered by local chiefs mostly belonging to the Rajput clans. At the end of the 13th century this territory was organised and ruled by a Hada Chauhan (Gupta, 1982: 25). The remaining history of the region under study is the story of conflict with neighbouring states as well as of ups and downs of one or another ruler for the sake of power. Therefore, least attention had been given to overall economic development. But in spite of political uncertainty and poor resource base several steps had been taken in various sectors of the economy, including marketing. Since this period was the initial period for the development of markets and marketing, whatever little development took place, has provided a base for the modern development of a market system.

During the medieval period, the then state capital Kota was the most important market centre of the region. Kota was interconnected with other State capitals as well as with adjoining townships. An important trade route Kabal to Khander passed through Kota and Bikaner. The main routes within the State were from Kota to Shahabad, Kota to Baran, Kota to Digod and from Shergarh to Kota via Gagron and Darrah. In fact, the origin of the present growth of marketing at Kota may be attributed to that period. Other settlements having limited retail market facilities were Sangod, Digod, Kaithun, Barod, Pipalod and Indergarh. During this period Kota State traded mostly with neighbouring States of Rajputana and

Central India. The opium of Kota State was claimed to be as good as, if not superior to, the Malwa product. It was manufactured in two shapes. That for the Chinese market, which was sent mostly to the government depot, was prepared in balls, while for home consumption or, for other states of Rajputana, it was made into cakes. Other exports were cereals, pulses, oilseeds, *ghee*, forest products, hides and Kota muslin. The main imports were sugar, *gur*, rice, tobacco, groceries, cloth, metals, dry fruits, leather goods and paper.

The practice of mobile trading was prevalent during those days both for collection and sale of necessary items. But it was completely unorganised and in the form of personal enterprise. Banjaras used to do this work. They moved in caravans so as to protect themselves from robberies. They carried goods like foodgrains, salt, sugar, cloth, etc., on bullocks and camels. There was also this system whereby a big trader proceeding on a commercial venture to a foreign country would have his intention proclaimed by beat of the drum and request other traders, if they so desired, to join him. Everyone went with his merchandise (*bhanda*), and traded on his own account, gaining or losing according to his own commercial acumen and enterprise (Tod, 1871: 492). The practice of announcement prior to the arrival of traders was common. It was the duty of the *Jagirdar* to protect the trader and if any trader suffered from theft or robbery on the way, the village where it was committed, was held responsible. The State also helped the trader if a purchaser refused to pay the cost of goods purchased. The banjaras had to pay a tax to the State. Long distance trading was also common for selected items.

An important feature of the medieval internal marketing system was the development of 'fairs' (*mela*) and 'weekly markets' (*hat bazar*) as trading institutions. These marketing institutions had been developed under the patronage of the royal chiefs. The old records of Kota State indicate that fairs were organised both for local and foreign trade. Realising the importance of fairs the rulers used to provide several organisational facilities to the traders. The *Hakim* of the *Pargana* was in charge of the fair and he was to go in person to arrange for the safety of the traders and their merchandise. At times, the ruler visited the fair in order to enhance its importance and also to honour the leading traders. It was the duty of the *hakim* to make arrangements for fodder or grass and water. A police station or *Kotwali Chabootra* was also established in the fair to maintain law and order during the period. While describing the Annals of Harouti Tod (1971: 129) has mentioned the occurrence of Sri Brij Nath Fair at Kota, the Sangod fair and Sitabari fair (now in Baran) as important fairs of Rajputana. The fairs of Chandkedi, Manoharthana, Sangod and Sitabari in Kota were meant specially for sale and purchase of bullocks and horses. Sometimes, tax concessions were also given to traders in order to induce them to participate in the fair.

The *hat* or locally known as *hatwara* is a weekly market, held once or twice a week and provide sale and purchase facilities to the respective areas. The development of '*hat bazar*' is a landmark of the medieval period, which still continues to provide trading facilities. These markets were organised at *Pargana* headquarters. On fixed market days, vendors and shopkeepers used to visit these markets with their goods (Sharma, 1979: 156).

The farmers, artisans and other producers of daily utility goods also sell their goods and purchase necessary items in these markets. Only a few references regarding the establishment or start of weekly markets in Rajasthan are available. In Kota State specific orders had been issued by the royal chiefs for the establishment of *hats*. Weekly markets were organised at all '*Pargana*' headquarters in the State. This was meant to provide facilities for sale and purchase to the neighbouring areas. Reasonable concessions and facilities were provided to shopkeepers (Bhandar No. 3 (Kota), Tilik Jagat Hukam Akham, V.S. (1958). With local patronage and popularity, weekly markets were started at all the important centres. In fact, the present network of weekly markets in the region under study owes its existence to the medieval period.

Apart from periodic markets, care was also taken to maintain the commercial importance of *mandis* as well as to promote new *mandis*. The traders of Rajgarh had established their business at Kota. The traders of important commercial cities were encouraged by the Regent of Kota to open their shops at Baran, Rampura, Mandawar, Jhalrapatan, Nandgaon and Suket. These traders were induced by facilities such as remission in taxes, assurance of protection, provision of land for their shops and houses and grant of loans, etc. Two main motives of all these concessions was to establish permanent *mandis* in the state. Thus, apart from Kota several market centres such as Indergarh, Piplod, Digod, Sultanpur, Sangod, Ramganjmandi had been developed as small market centres. In brief, local rulers encouraged local as well as foreign trade by organising fairs at different centres, *hat* bazar for local needs and establishment of permanent commercial *mandis*.

Modern Period

This period can be divided into two sub-periods: (i) British period, and (ii) post-independence period.

(i) British Period: The British period of Indian history may be considered as a period of the exploitation of resources, that too for the sake of foreign trade. But at the same time, this was also a period of the beginning of economic development in sectors like transportation, communication, agriculture, mining and marketing. A structural change was taking place in the spheres of agricultural production, crop pattern and marketing. Kota State came into contact with the Britishers through a treaty between Maharao of Kota and the British East India Company in December 1817. By this treaty Kota was taken under the protection of the British government. During this period emphasis was given to the construction of roads and

bridges. The opening of the railway line in 1906 between Kota-Baran-Guna and in 1908 between Mathura-Nagda via Kota was a landmark in trade and commerce activity of this region. Apart from this nothing substantial had been done, although local authorities were engaged in the usual developmental activities. The local, regional and terminal market centres for various commodities were established. But the marketing system was unchanged and the marketable surpluses of the majority of the producer-sellers were meagre. The farmers were at the mercy of money-lenders and various malpractices in selling method, price fixation, weight, payment, quality, market allowances, market charges, accounts, etc., were prevalent. The trade in *mandis* were developed and more retail outlets established by local shopkeepers in order to fulfil the needs of the people.

(ii) Post-independence Period: The British rule in India ended in 1947 and with the formation of the Indian Republic, there was an urgent need to formulate new economic policies for the country as a whole as well as for each State. In March 1948, nine states including Kota formed Rajasthan (former) with Kota as its capital. This union was merged into the United States of Greater Rajasthan and later into Rajasthan. Kota district, including the present Baran district, was carved out in 1949 with Kota town as district headquarters.

After independence, there has been a rapid transformation of economic conditions and planned development was started with the implementation of the First Five Year Plan from April 1951. In the field of marketing special emphasis was given to agricultural marketing. The need for the establishment of regulated markets was felt because the prevailing system was not suitable, especially to producer farmers. Oligopolistic buying, underhand dealings in terms of bids and offers, various malpractices including overweighing, manipulation of accounts, delayed payments, unwarranted compulsory deduction, etc., resulted in the exploitation of farmers. Thus, under the

Rajasthan Agricultural Marketing Act, 1961, regulated markets were established in the form of 'Krishi Upaj Mandi Samiti'. These markets not only provide trading facilities but also develop market yards with all types of modern facilities for agriculture marketing. In the region under study regulated markets at Kota, Ramganjmandi and Sumerganjmandi were established in January 1964.

After independence market centres especially market towns have been developed rapidly. Both retail and wholesale marketing became important. Kota city, the largest town of Central Hadaoti was developed as a major trade centre not only of the region but also of the State. This process is still continuing and now Kota is having a complex system of marketing with several market centres within the city. The other market centres of the region are Ramganjmandi, Morak, Dara, Suket, Sangod, Ladpura, Digod, Sultanpur, Itawa, Piplod, Sumerganjmandi and Indergarh.

The rural marketing in the region is still traditional with the dominance of *hat bazar* (weekly markets) and fairs supported by mobile traders. The growth of permanent shops and small markets are a part of the regular development process. In brief, the present marketing system of the region under study is a combination of modern and traditional marketing. Both these systems happily co-exist because of their adoptivity with the regional ecosystem.

Growth of Marketing System and Markets and the Ecological Complex

The growth and development of markets and marketing system, as described above are in a state of continuous change and their characteristics are not only attributable to present day economic factors, but also to historical legacies and to socio-cultural factors. A few studies have been done regarding the origin and growth of marketing systems, but no conceptual schemata have been devised to account for major changes in market systems, disappearance of market days or establishment of new market centres. The ecological approach, as applied by Symanski and Bromley (1974) for the growth of Andean markets can be used to explain the growth of marketing system in developing countries, including that of the region under study.

The Ecological Complex

An ecological complex is a system of four interrelated clusters of variables—environment, embracing both natural conditions and man-made landscape; population, expressed in terms of distribution, density and demographic structure; organisation, including economic and social institutions and the patterns of socio-economic interactions; and technology. "This ecological complex has been related to such important ecological processes as competition, collaboration, succession, dominance, invasion, differentiation and spatial interaction" (Symanski and Bromley, 1974: 382). The environmental change, changes in size and composition of population and introduction of new technology are interrelated and is responsible for changes in socio-economic processes including that of the marketing system.

A Framework for Explanation

The ecological complex with its associated ecological process provides a basis for the growth and changes in markets and marketing system. Figure 3.2 shows the nature of changes in market systems stimulated by technological changes specially that of transport improvements and relationship with ecological complex as developed by Symanski and Bromley (1974).

As shown in the figure, the changes in market systems are initially triggered off by improvements in transport technology. These changes tend to a greater demand of goods that readjusts the market system. Similarly, population growth tends to cause increased spatial interaction, leading to greater competition, and to the reorganisation of market activities. In this process, environment (physical and man-made) plays a key role in developing the economic landscape including market organisations.

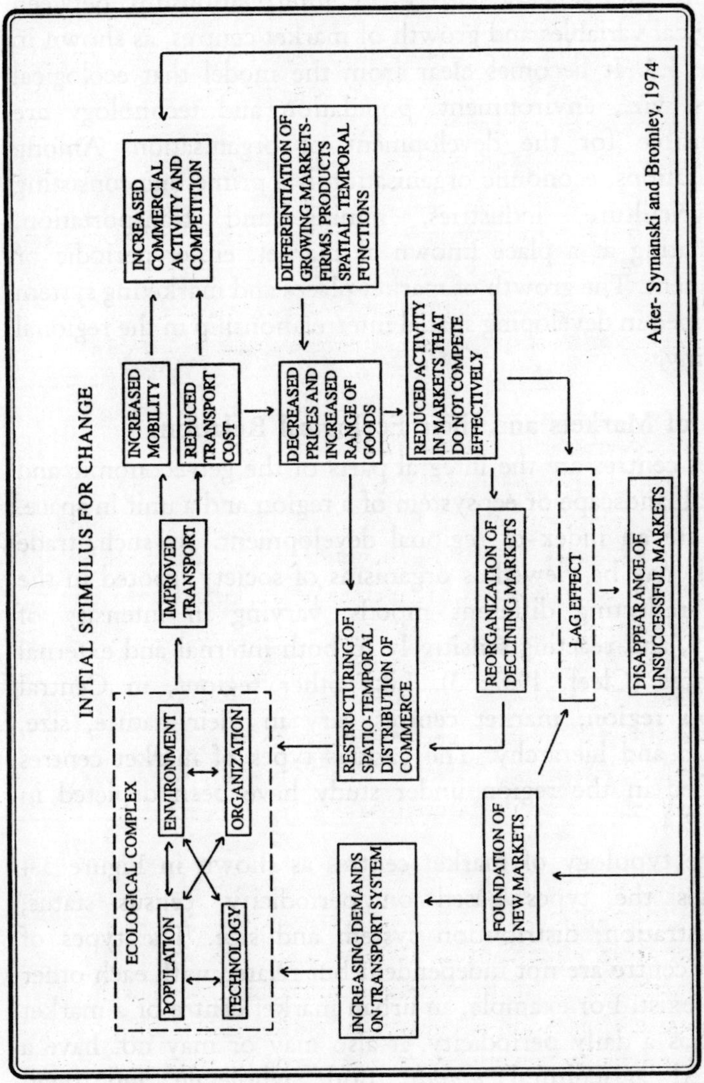

Figure 3.2
Ecological Complex and Market Systems

A simplified framework of the ecological complex and growth of markets has been used by Saxena (1990: 28), which explains the general pattern of interrelationship between ecological variables and growth of market centres, as shown in Figure 3.3. It becomes clear from the model that ecological factors, viz., environment, population and technology are responsible for the development of organisation. Among organisations, economic organisation is a prime one consisting of agriculture, industries, mining and transportation, culminating at a place known as market, either periodic or permanent. The growth of market-places and marketing system has helped in developing spatial interrelationship in the regional economy.

Types of Markets and their Ecological Relations

Market centres are the integral parts of the geo-economic and cultural landscape or ecosystem of a region and a unit in space. They are an index of regional development. As such, trade centres may be viewed as organisms of society, rooted in the earth, reflecting different moods, varying in intensity of activity, and reacting sensitively to both internal and external influences (Cleef, 1937: 3). Like other regions, in Central Hadaoti region, market centres vary in their nature, size, function and hierarchy. The various types of market centres identified in the region under study have been depicted in Figure 3.4.

The typology of market centres as shown in Figure 3.4 indicates the types based on periodicity, census status, administration, distribution system and size. The types of market centre are not independent but related with each other and co-exist. For example, an urban market centre or a market town has a daily periodicity, it also may or may not have a regulated agricultural *mandi*. Both wholesale and retail marketing are integral parts of a marketing system. Kota city is a good example having all the characteristics, including *hat*

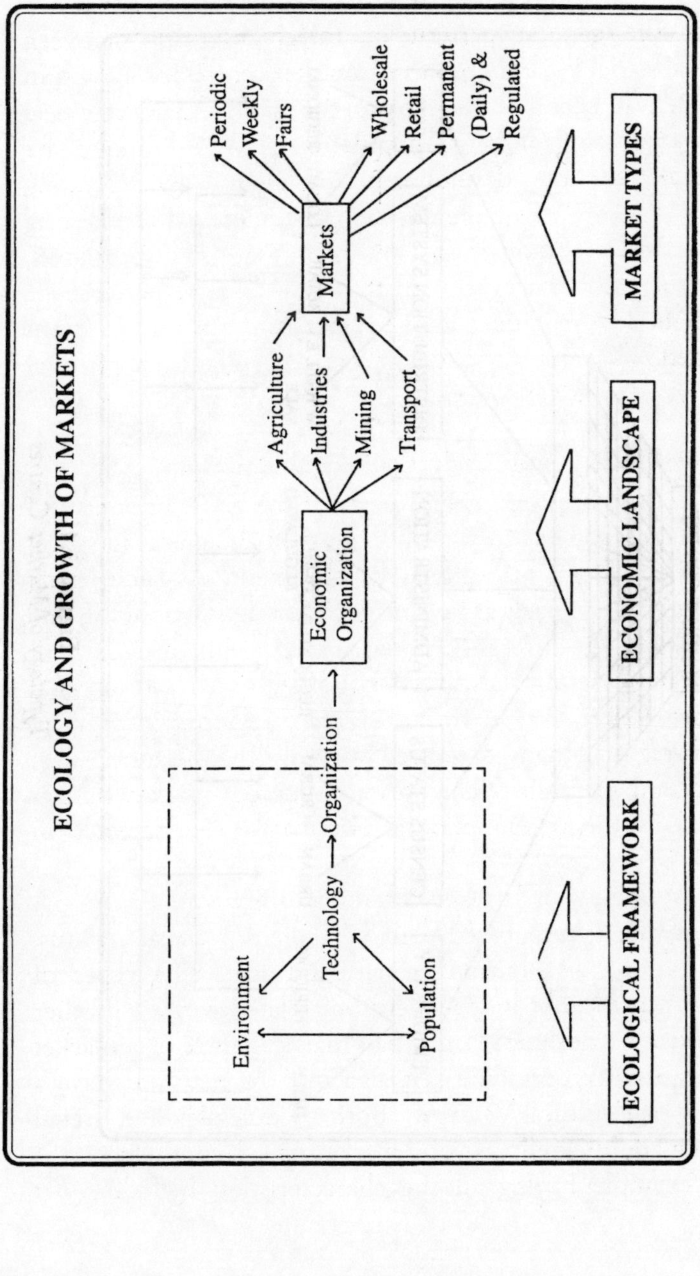

Figure 3.3
Ecology and Growth of Markets

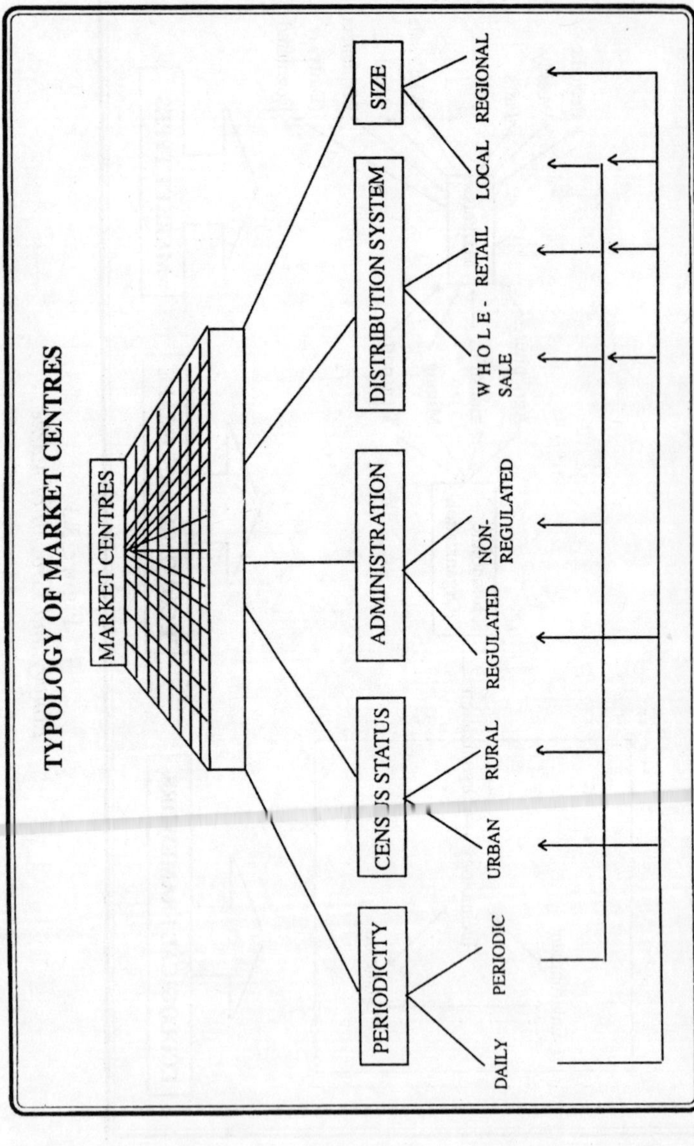

Figure 3.4
Typology of Market Centres

bazar (periodic market) also. Therefore, the above classification is only for a general understanding of the marketing system. The basic types of market centre/marketing system include:

(i) Periodic markets
  (a) Weekly markets
  (b) Fairs

(ii) Market Towns including agricultural *mandis*

The ecological complex with its associated ecological processes provide an invaluable basis for growth, development and success of the entire marketing system. The nature of an individual market system can be explained by the four interdependent clusters of variables in the ecological complex—market organisation; the cluster of socio-economic organisation, which change according to changes in variables of population; technology; and general socio-economic organisation and environment.

The growth and development of markets as a reflection of the ecological adjustment and the existence of various forms of marketing is also due to environmental conditions of the region. Periodic markets had been developed in regions where population was limited, economy was simple mostly subsistence, means of transportation was limited and environmental conditions were harsh and not favourable for permanent marketing. The growth of the 'fair' was in total adjustment with the ecosystem. The occurrence of the fair, once or twice in a year is a reflection of very limited demand and surplus available for sale. The schedule of fairs was fixed with the climatic conditions and timings of harvest of crops. Many fairs are still held on festival days. The occurrence of cattle fairs in the region is an indicator of the importance of cattle in the regional economy. In all, there are 48 fairs held in the Central Hadaoti region.

The growth of market towns and agricultural *mandis* are also determined by physical or environmental factors. All the market towns are not *mandis* but some of them have attained the status of regulated markets. In the region under study, there are seven urban centres and five regulated markets. Kota is the urban centre in its real form, where all types of urban facilities are available. Located on the bank of river Chambal, Kota has a well developed market infrastructure including a regulated '*mandi*'. The relief, climate, availability of water and productive land have helped it to develop as a leading market centre not only of the region but of the entire State. The other markets like Ramganjmandi, Sangod, Itawa, Sumerganjmandi, Kaithoon, Suket and Sultanpur have also developed due to their favourable geo-economic conditions. The growth of agricultural markets in the region had been determined by environmental factors but technological factors have also played a determining role.

Apart from the above mentioned marketing systems, there are village markets, where limited exchange of commodities, mostly of daily consumable items, took place. These markets are in the form of village shops mostly located at some prime location in the village. The practice of mobile traders is also common in the region. The mobile traders used to visit rural areas in an individual capacity with a particular type of goods such as cloth, plastic goods, cosmetics and other luxury items for women, etc. The mobility and frequency of these traders very much depended upon climatic conditions, relief and mode of transport. During the rainy season their frequency is low, while it increases during the winters. During the process of ecological changes, individual markets adjust either by reorganisation and/or disappearance. Some unsuccessful markets may disappear but mostly they adjust by reorganisation. In the region under study the process of reorganisation can be seen in periodic markets, which are still continuing successfully in spite of rapid urbanisation. This has become possible because periodic markets are an integral part of the social ecology of the region. In brief, the regional marketing pattern of Central Hadaoti is the result of the changing interrelationship between man-environment-technology and organisation, or in other words the ecological complex.

References

Balshaw, C.S. (1965), *Traditional Exchange and Modern Markets*, Prentice Hall of India, New Delhi.

Berry, B.J.L. (1967), *Geography of Market Centres and Retail Distribution*, Prentice Hall.

Chattopadhyaya, S. (1958), *Early History of North India*, Calcutta.

Cleef, E.V. (1937), *Trade Centres and Trade Routes*, D. Appleton-Century Co., New York.

Gupta, Savitri (1982), *Rajasthan District Gazetteers*, Kota, Jaipur.

Hodder, B.W. and Lee, Rojer (1974), *Economic Geography*, Methuen, London.

Majumdar, R.C. (1957), *The History and Culture of the Indian People*, Bombay.

Mulvihill, D.F. and Mulvihill, R.C. (1970), *Geography, Marketing and Urban Growth*, Van Nostrand.

Pirenne, H. (1936), *Economic and Social History of Medieval Europe*, New York.

Polanyi, K. (1957), *Trade and Markets in Early Empires*, Glencoe.

Saxena, H.M. (1990), *Marketing Geography*, Rawat Publications, Jaipur.

Sharma, G.S. (1979), *Administrative System of the Rajputs*, Rajesh Publications, New Delhi.

Symanski, R. and Bromley, R.J. (1974), Market Development and the Ecological Complex, *Professional Geographer*, Vol. 26, No. 4, pp. 382-388.

Tod, James (1971), *Annals and Antiquities of Rajasthan*, K.M.N. Pub., New Delhi.

Tripathi, Rama Shankar (1969), *History of Ancient India*, Delhi.

Chapter 4

Urban Markets and Marketing

Marketing activity and market institutions are ubiquitous to urban development. Economically defined, the city is a settlement, the inhabitants of which live primarily off trade and commerce rather than agriculture (Welaer, 1958: 65-66). Thus, every city and town, from metropolitan to small is engaged in and is at least partially, supported by marketing activities. In some towns trade and commerce activity become more important than others, such towns can be termed as 'market towns'. Marketing, then, plays a pivotal role in the development and growth of a region. Another significant aspect of urban marketing is its impact on environment. The assessment of the impact of urban marketing can only be done by unfolding the geographical nature and development of urban markets in the region under study, for which the present chapter has been designed.

While economic geographers have given much attention to the study of resources and factors of production, they have neglected their associated market centres. With the growing interest among geographers it was claimed during the 1960s that marketing geography had 'come of age'. William Applebaum (1954: 246), the chief architect of marketing geography, has stated its main concern as being "with the delinitation and measurement of markets and with the channels of distribution through which the goods move from producer to consumer". The pattern of relationship between marketing and urban growth has been discussed by Mulvihill and Mulvihill (1967) in their book entitled, *Geography, Marketing and Urban Growth*. Berry (1963, 1965, 1967) has presented a systematic account of the commercial structure of urban markets. Alam (1963), Gopal Krishan and Agarwal (1973), Saxena (1974, 1978-79) and Sami (1980) have described the commercial structure of cities of Hyderabad-Secunderabad, Chandigarh, Kota, Sriganganagar and Patna, respectively, while the retail marketing pattern has been discussed in detail by Berry (1967) and Peter Scott (1970). Ross L. Davies' work entitled *Marketing Geography* (1977) is also a notable work. In brief, urban marketing patterns and the study of city commercial land use as well as shopping patterns, etc., have become a popular subject of research in urban and marketing geography. Not only foreign geographers but Indian geographers have also done notable research. Several Ph.D. dissertations (mostly unpublished) completed in the University Departments of Geography at Gorakhpur, Varanasi, Udaipur, Patna and Rajasthan have discussed various aspects of urban marketing.

Identification and Distribution of Market Towns

The identification of market towns is one of the basic problems in marketing geography. A range of measures have been applied to differentiation of towns, urban centres, central places, growth centres; but so far no criteria have been evolved and certainly none accepted generally for differentiation of market towns. Can all the 'census towns' be considered as 'market towns'? Urban centres do have marketing facilities but there are small settlements which do not have even market infrastructures, but are included as urban centres because they fulfil the following conditions laid down for urban centres:

(i) minimum population of 5,000,
(ii) 75 per cent of its male working population are pursuing non-agricultural activity, and
(iii) inhabitated by at least 400 persons per sq.km.

Accordingly, in Central Hadaoti, the following urban centres have been identified in 1991 census:

Table 4.1
Urban Centres of Kota District, 1991

Urban Centres	*Population*
1. Kota	5,37,371
2. Kaithoon	16,040
3. Udaipura	6,073
4. Ramganjmandi	20,875
5. Satalkheri	9,742
6. Suket	11,056
7. Sangod	15,603

Our survey reveals that Udaipura and Satalkheri are the mining centres but do not have market infrastructures. Even the number of retail shops are less than 20, therefore these cannot be termed as 'market towns'.

Another view is that market towns are, presumably, towns with market-places (institutionalised). Some settlements may not be census towns but have retail/wholesale marketing functions and also have market infrastructures. Such centres can be included as market towns. In the region under study Itawa, Sultanpur and Sumerganjmandi are centres which can be termed as 'market towns'. The population of Itawa and Sultanpur was 12,193 and 10,175 respectively in 1991. Itawa and Sumerganjmandi also have agricultural regulated markets. All these centres have retail/wholesale marketing as well as banking, insurance and other facilities. Thus, for the present study, the following centres have been identified as market towns: 1. Kota, 2. Ramganjmandi, 3. Sangod, 4.

Kaithoon, 5. Suket, 6. Itawa, 7. Sultanpur and 8. Sumerganjmandi (Fig. 4.1).

Since the number of market towns in the region is very limited (8 only), the distributional pattern is also very simple. Kota, Ramganjmandi and Piplod tehsils have two market towns each, while Sangod and Digod tehsils have one market town each. Apart from Kota, Kaithoon town is located in Kota tehsil, similarly Ramganjmandi and Suket are located in Ramganjmandi tehsil. Piplod tehsil has Itawa and Sumerganjmandi, Digod have Sultanpur and Sagod is in Sangod tehsil. All the market towns are well distributed in the region and serve as sale and purchase centres. The distributional pattern is so simple (as shown in Fig. 4.1) that there is no need for any statistical analysis.

Location of Market Towns in Relation to Geo-economic Factors

The factor of location is seen as one in which the geographical influence stands out most prominently. The locational factor not only exercises its influence on the growth of a town as a market centre, but it also acts and reacts incessantly from the stage when a replacement begins to the stage when it acquires the status of a market town. While dealing with locational analysis, let us state that the present analysis is based on factors responsible for growth and development of market towns, rather than on theoretical models based on central place studies. The location of market towns in the region under study is influenced by the following important factors:

(i) transportation,
(ii) market towns as 'break-of-bulk' centres,
(iii) agricultural land use, and
(iv) surrounding villages and population.

(i) Transportation

Transportation is a determining factor of the location of market towns. Transport facilities generally determine the degree of

Figure 4.1
Market Towns of Central Hadaoti

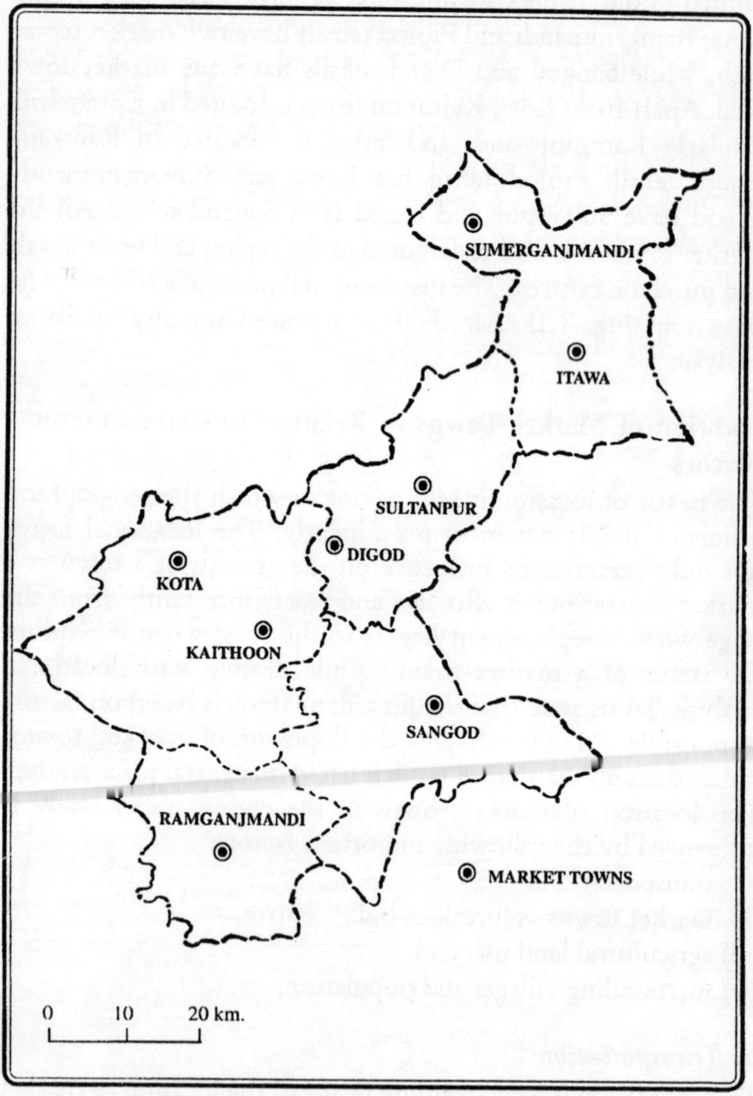

accessibility of a given centre. Thus, trade, transportation and market development are interdependent phenomena. In other words, an easy access to a trade centre is paramount to its vigorous growth. Market transport relationship also brings forth a concept known as static and dynamic areas. A region becomes more explicitly dynamic when proper transportation facilities are available. The functional aspect of a region generally is the product of interaction among settlements, areal economy and also lines of transportation. If any of these three variables are absent and do not form part of the interaction, the given area or region ceases to be functional, it becomes static. Market centres which are essentially meeting points both of consumers and of regional goods structure become dynamic as has expressed by Mukerjee (1968: 102). "Landscape and culture has its static and dynamic ecological aspects. Crops, goods and men in movement represent the dynamic elements of the social-ecological situation".

The hypothesis that the key component of market location is the availability of transportation has been examined. Our study reveals that market towns are located at the point of 'route convergence' or at the 'cross-road nodes'. The nature of route convergence at market towns in Central Hadaoti has been depicted in Figure 4.2 and also given in Table 4.2.

Table 4.2

Route Convergence at Market Towns in Central Hadaoti

Market Towns	*Nature of Route Convergence*
1. Kota	Railway junction; 6 metalled roads including NH 12
2. Ramganjmandi	Four metalled roads
3. Sangod	Four metalled roads
4. Suket	Four metalled roads
5. Kaithoon	Roadside location
6. Itawa	Four metalled roads
7. Sultanpur	Three metalled roads
8. Sumerganjmandi	Railway station and two metalled roads

Figure 4.2
Central Hadaoti: Nature of Route Convergence

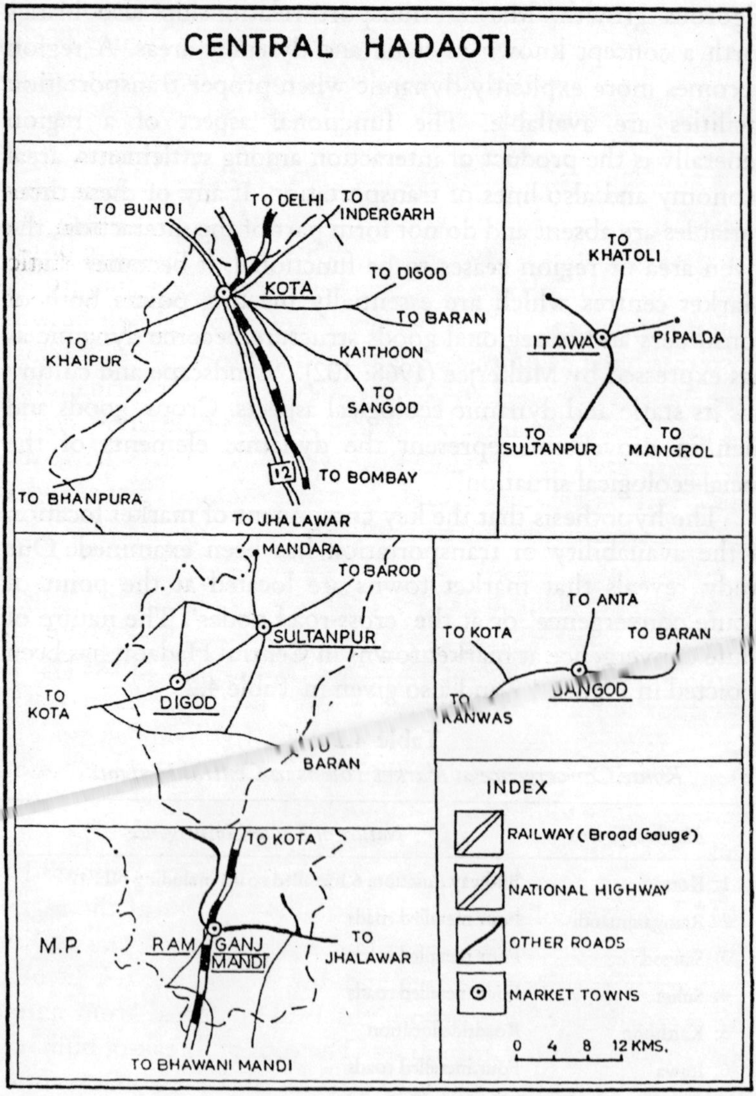

It becomes clear from Figure 4.2 and the above table that all the market towns of the region are having transport route convergence location. Except Kaithoon which has a road-side location, all other market towns have 'cross-road node' location. Only three towns, viz., Kota, Ramganjmandi and Sumerganjmandi have railway facilities. Among them Kota is a railway junction with the highest degree of connectivity in the region. Other market towns are still small but are growing.

(ii) Market Towns as 'Break-of-bulk' Centres

Another important aspect determining the location and growth of market centres is whether it is a break-of-bulk centre or not. There are certain centres which come into being and grow at the points where bulk is broken at the border town between two dissimilar regions. As a general hypothesis, market centres preferably select lines of contact among different formations—either relief, structure, areal economy or even different systems of transportation Therefore, 'break-of-bulk' centres are located either: (i) on the borderland of two dissimilar regions, and/or (ii) where the mode of transport is changed.

In Central Hadaoti region all the market towns are located at the point where bulk is broken due to change in mode of transport. Cleef (1937: 10) has rightly observed that where shift in load is effected, owing to a necessary change in the type of transport medium or any other reason, trade centres may arise. In the region under study, a change of two dissimilar modes of transport has been seen in the form of head-load and animal carts to automobiles, and automobiles to railways. Kota is the best example of it, where agricultural, mining and other products are collected and then exported to other regions. This is the biggest collecting and distributing centre of the region. Ramganjmandi and Sumerganjmandi also have railway facilities and act as smaller collecting and distributing centres. In other market towns of the region, the load is shifted from animal driven vehicles to automobiles. The case of 'break-of-bulk' due to change of relief, is not very obvious in the region, except for

Kota, Ramganjmandi and Suket which are located at the contact point of hilly and plain regions.

(iii) Agricultural Land Use and Location of Market Towns

Market towns owe their existence to surplus agricultural production which is available for trade. The need for provision of adequate facilities for marketing agricultural produce has been a major motivating force in market town development. Among market towns of the region five towns are primary agricultural regulated markets. These are Kota, Itawa, Ramganjmandi, Sangod and Sumerganjmandi, while Sultanpur, Suket and Kaithoon are having sub-yards. Kota is a 'Super A class' mandi followed by Ramganjmandi. All other market towns are of smaller size. But it becomes clear that agricultural production, especially surplus production is responsible for the growth of marketing activities in market towns of the Central Hadaoti region.

(iv) Location in Relation to Surrounding Villages

Market towns are always functionally related to the countryside or villages. They provide an opportunity for marketing of agricultural products and also serve as retail and/or service centres. The proper interaction between urban centres and surrounding rural areas is vital for the growth and development of market towns. A study conducted by NCAER, 'Market Towns and Spatial Development in India' highlighted the fact that in India one market town is located for 295 villages as compared to one market town for every 11 or 12 villages in USA. In Rajasthan as a whole, one market town is available for 416 villages. However, in the region under study the situation is satisfactory in comparison to the state as well as the rest of the country. The total number of villages are 811, therefore, each market towns on an average serves nearly 100 villages. Apart from these there are some rural markets also which serve as rural marketing centres.

Market Morphology/Infrastructures

Markets are the significant dynamic elements in which are inherent the expression of cultural and economic structures of the region. They have an internal geography of their own, termed as Market Morphology. The morphological pattern of a market town is a complex areal phenomenon consisting of the features of market-places, or in other words, market infrastructures. It is a reflection not of the immediate and current space requirements of the community but rather of their cumulative needs over a period of years. The morphology of a market is the result of the physical environment on the one hand and the social and political conditions on the other. The study of the morphological pattern is not only necessary to understand the present pattern but also to provide a guideline for planning and investment in facilities, merchandise and promotional activities. Many geographers have studied market infrastructures. The studies conducted by Proudfoot (1937), Berry (1963, 1965, 1967), Alam (1963), Gopal Krishan and Agarwal (1973), Saxena (1978-79), etc., have given a direction for further study. The study of market morphology, in the present context, is also necessary to explain the ecological framework of marketing and its impact on urban environment.

Growth and Components of Market Morphology

Every market town has its own morphology, which forms an integral part of the urban morphology, also known as 'commercial land use' of the city. The commercial land use in the city means the space used for the commercial purposes, i.e., retail and wholesale markets, storage, agricultural *mandi*, banks, insurance, etc. The growth of market morphology is directly linked with the growth of a settlement and it is very difficult to find out whether the 'marketing activity determines the man-made geographic structure or whether the structure of the urban area determines the marketing activity' (Mulvihill & Mulvihill, 1970: 74). In fact, both these factors are interrelated and interdependent. The Central Hadaoti region is a good example of the theory that market morphological patterns become more complex as towns grow in size. In the region under study there are market towns like Kaithoon, Suket, Sangod, Itawa, Sultanpur, Sumerganjmandi, which have a very simple market morphology. In these towns shops are located either along the main road of the town or at main the cross road point locally known as *choraha*. A developed but simple market morphological pattern can be seen at Ramganjmandi, a small town of about 25,000 population. On the other hand Kota is the biggest market town of the region with a complex market morphology.

The components of market morphology have been described by several geographers, most of them from developed countries, and their studies are therefore related to the large cities of USA and West Europe. In the context of Rajasthan, Saxena (1999: 92) has described the following typology of the market morphology:

Typology of the Components of Market Morphology
(For towns having more than 50,000 population)

Primary Components	*Secondary Components*
I Central Business Area	(a) Mixed retail zone
	(b) Wholesale zone
	(c) Regional centres
II Secondary Business Area	(a) Retail shops
	(b) Wholesale zone
III Principal Business Arteries	(a) Retail shops
	(b) Service-cum-sale shops
	(c) Service shops
IV Connecting Business Streets	(a) Grocers shops
	(b) Furniture row
	(c) Vegetable and fruits row
	(d) Auto-repair shops
	(e) Drug (medical) stores
	(f) Other specialised shops

Contd...

Contd...

V Isolated clusters	(a) Commodity stores
	(b) Service stores
	(c) Mixed stores
For towns having 15,000 to 50,000 population	
I Central Business street	(a) Retail shops
	(b) Wholesale shops
II Main Business Street	(a) Retail shops
III Connecting Business Streets	Grocers, Furnitures, Service-cum sale shops.
For towns having less than 15,000 population	
I Main Business Street and/or	
II Adjoining Business street	Mixed retail shops
III Isolated shops	

In Central Hadaoti region Kota is the only market town having a well developed market morphological pattern (its detailed analysis has been done in sample study). Among other market towns Ramganjmandi also has a systematic development of market infrastructure, but all the other remaining towns possess only a main street as the business street and some isolated clusters of shops.

General Characteristics of Morphological Components of Market Towns in Central Hadaoti

Central Business Area

The Central Business Area is similar to the CBD but without some of the characteristics described by foreign geographers. It represents the retail heart of the town with facilities of wholesale marketing. Banks and insurance companies are also located in this area. In fact, it is the centre of retail and wholesale marketing of the city and plays a vital role in commercial activities. In market towns of Central Hadaoti, Kota city is the only city having a central business area located in Rampura-Bajaj Khana area. But now concentration is shifting towards

Chawani Choraha-Gumanpura area. Ramganjmandi has its CBA at Railway Station towards Number 4 crossroad. In all other towns the 'main bazar' may be considered as its central business area.

Secondary Business Area

The SBA is a characteristic of big market towns and develops in order to fulfil the needs of a growing population. Its nature is more or less similar to that of CBA, but both its volume of trade and expansion is limited. At Kota, the SBA has been developed at Railway Junction (Bhimmandi), Gumanpura, Chawani, Choraha Nayapura. In other market towns of the region the SBA does not exist.

Principal Business Street and Connecting Business Streets

The principal business street is a characteristic of all the market towns, while connecting business streets can be seen in big towns only. Such streets contain retail shops, service-cum-sale shops and service shops only. A variety of stores exist there and serve the local as well as adjoining areas. Connecting business streets are those streets which are connected with the main street. They are characterised by the presence of several types of shops such as furniture, grocery, readymade garments, cloth, vegetable and fruits, medical stores, etc. All the market towns of the region have the principal business street as main market or bada bazar with mixed type of shops. Connecting business streets exist in Kota only.

Isolated Clusters and Shops

These are characteristically found in all categories of towns. In towns with more than 50,000 population their number is more, as in the case of Kota city, where more than fifty clusters are distributed throughout the town. In other towns a few clusters serve the needs of local residents. In very small towns like Suket, Sangod, Itawa, Sumerganjmandi, Sultanpur, Kaithoon only isolated shops provide retail marketing facility. These shops are mostly located either in the outskirts of the town or in residential areas.

As described in the above analysis, Kota is the only market town where market infrastructures have developed well and all the components of market morphology are present. Therefore, a sample study of the market morphology of Kota has been conducted. The details of the study are as follows:

Sample Study of the Market Morphology of Kota City

Kota (78°10'E; 23°11'N) is a regional market situated in the south-eastern part of Rajasthan and forms a part of the physiographic region known as the 'Madhya Bharat Pathar' at the junction of the plateau and the Chambal valley. Its location at an elevation of about 250 m is remarkable in the sense that it commands the Chambal at the point where it leaves the plateau to flow in the valley-plains of its own and river Kalisindh. The site of Kota is of considerable importance being the fertile riverine tract of the Chambal in the north and sandstone outcrops in the south. The significance of the site may thus be characterised simultaneously by three-fold advantages of water, defence and nodality. It is largely because of the potentialities of its geographical site that Kota has grown into one of the leading industrial towns not only of Rajasthan but of the entire country.

Nature of Origin and Subsequent Growth of Market Morphology

It is said that in the 14th century, some Bhils of 'Koteah' clan were residing here, and were attacked and ousted by Jet Singh, the grandson of Rao Dewa of Bundi, who settled in the place, and built a town which is called 'Kotah'. It is clear from the historical records that the nucleus of the city initially came into existence in areas of Kethonee Pol-Retwali and Radha-Bilas. Later on during the reign of Kishore Singh (1664-96),

Kishorepura was inhabited and a tank now known as Kishore Sagar, and also a royal palace were constructed. This reveals that the nucleus of Kota city originated around Kishorepura and along the Chambal from south to north which later on grew into a triangle with a base extending from Kishorepura to Gumanpura and an apex at Ladpura. It was during the period 1696-1706 AD that Rampura market developed at the northern end in a linear form between habitations, and with the gradual increase of population the residential area spread out east and northward, within the town wall. It was during 1765-71 AD that a small section settled outside the eastern part of the town wall known as Gumanpura. In the year 1788 a cattle-cum-commodity fair was started annually which was later known as the 'Dashera Fair'. This is continued even to this day and is one of the biggest fairs of Rajasthan. During 1800-1900 the growth of the town was further intensified and several markets like Old Dhanmandi, Bajaj Khana, Ghantaghar were developed within the walled town area. Another phase in the development of market morphology of Kota was brought about with the coming up of railway line in 1907. The origin of Bhimganj Mandi near the railway junction, which is primarily a commercial trade centre, was largely because of the availability of transport facilities. The post-independence phase of the growth of the market morphology of Kota includes the markets of Nayapura and Gumanpura as well as further development in the Bhimganj Mandi area. Later on and more recently the growth includes the industrial estate, newly developed grain-*mandi* which is an improvement over the old one, and a new shopping centre at Gumanpura.

Market-Places of Kota

It is the market-place which actually links people of various residential areas within the city to areas of retail as well as wholesale establishments. This relationship is meaningful in many ways like form, function and evolution of a city or in other words, it explains the spatial behaviour of markets and residential areas within a market. Broadly speaking, there are four main types of market-places comprising the market morphology of Kota. These are:

(i) The Central Business Area,
(ii) The principal business thoroughfare,
(iii) The neighbourhood business street, and
(iv) The isolated store-clusters.

The Central Business Area (CBA) represents the retail heart of the city. Here, individual as well as collective retail stores do a greater volume of business per unit area than elsewhere in the market. It is here that the retail stores occupy choice street level frontage and there are large departmental stores, furniture stores, shoe stores, jewellery and other establishments selling goods. The upper storey of the establishment in some cases is occupied by offices, while occupance is restricted to some scattered hotels. In this area stores of subordinate importance like drug and tobacco, chemical stores and other stores selling convenience goods are located. The Central Business Area of Kota, like the business area of any other Indian town, may not have all the aforesaid characteristics. For instance, it does not have such buildings where the upper storey is occupied by service-establishments or offices, but on the contrary, it is largely used for residential purposes. Rampura, the so-called CBA of Kota, is the main retail heart of the city and draws its customers from all parts of the city proper and also from neighbouring smaller towns and villages. It is here that a large number of general stores, banks, furniture and chemical stores, shoe stores, ready-made garments stores, radio, electrical goods stores and jewellery stores, etc., are concentrated. Besides these, there are some shops of secondary importance selling medicines, newspapers, stationery and books, and there are some restaurants also.

The CBA of Kota is a principal business thoroughfare, characterised by the existence of a business-street running from

Figure 4.3
Market Places of Kota City

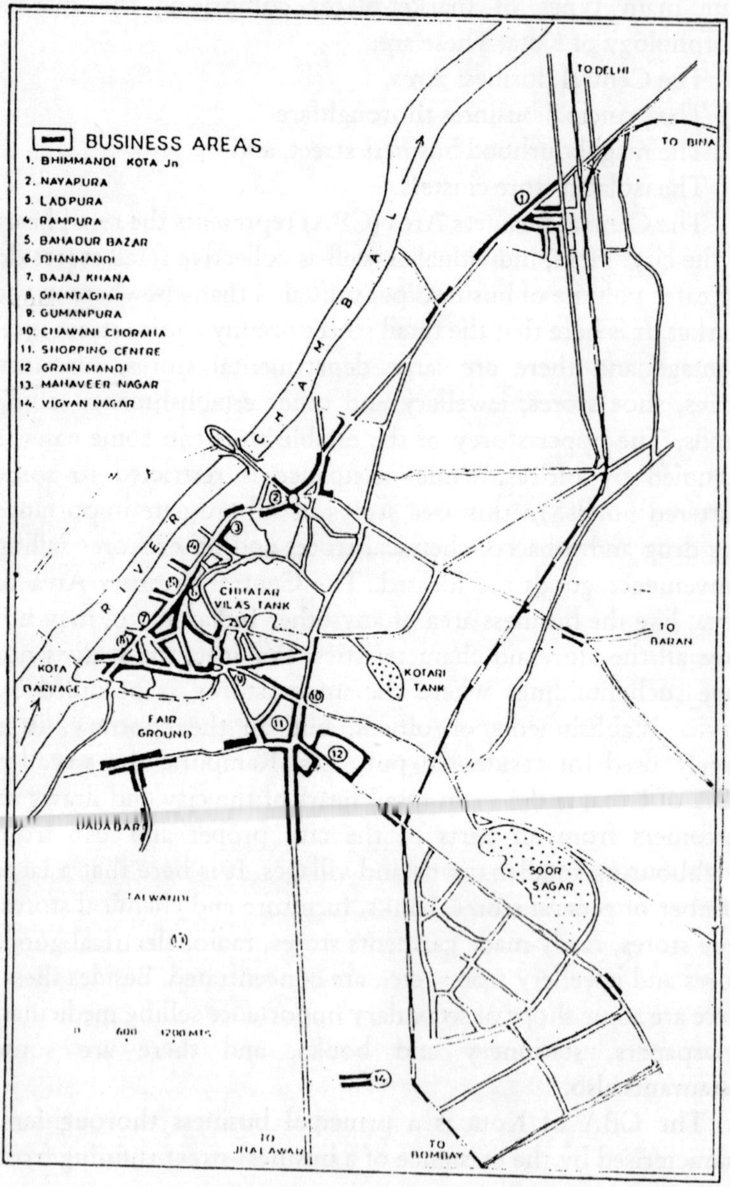

Nayapura to Patan Pole including retail markets of Ladpura, Rampura, Bhadur Bazar, Bajajkhana, Ghantaghar Chowk, Chothmata bazar, etc. It is both a business and a traffic artery. It runs right through the central business area and includes both specialised and general markets. The specialised markets include Bajaj-Khana for cloth, Chothmata Bazar also known as 'Sarafa Bazar' for silver and gold ornaments. Rest of the markets are characterised by the presence of mixed retail structures.

There are some tributary business streets converging at the principal business thoroughfare. These business streets are narrow and generally have markets of vegetables, foodgrains, kasara, miscellaneous products, clothes, etc. These include Subzimandi, Dhanmandi, Arya-Samaj Road, Behrugali, etc.

The neighbourhood business streets are situated at some distance from principal business thoroughfare, and these serve mainly the areas outside the city wall. Two such markets, Bhimganj Mandi and Gumanpura have multifunctional structures. The Bhimganj Mandi is approximately at a distance of five kms. from the walled city and is separated from it by the Civil Lines and administrative buildings. But the Gumanpura business street is quite close to the wall. Both these markets consist of rows of large and small shops or stalls dealing in a variety of goods like grocery and general merchandise, cloth store, *kirana* or provisions stores, fruits and confectionery stalls, electrical goods and a few service establishments like shops of barbers, dry-cleaners, tailors, etc. The neighbourhood business streets draw their customers mainly from easy walking distance, i.e., from surrounding locality or *mohallas*.

Among the isolated store clusters, Bundi Bus Stand, Chawani Choraha, Tipta, Sripura, Vigyan Nagar, Dadabadi, Talwandi, Mahaveer Nagar, Baran Road and Sriram colony are important. These are actually points where a few general stores or small restaurants have come up serving people going out or coming into the city. In fact, every locality now has a few shops.

Shopping Centres and Wholesale Markets

Kota is a regional commercial market not only of the Hadaoti but of the entire Rajasthan State. The development of shopping centres of hierarchical order is a characteristic feature of the town. These centres can be divided into four categories, as under:

1.	Central Business Area and Sub-City centre	Regional and city level
2.	District Centres and Sub-District Centres	District level
3.	Local Shopping Centres	Local level
4.	Convenient (Corner) Shops	Local level

As described earlier, the central business area is located in the walled city. A new business area is developing in the Gumanpura shopping centre. Bhimmandi, Chawani Choraha, Nayapura, Areodrum circle and Krishi Upaj Mandi have been developed as sub-city centres. A number of district centres have been developed in different parts of the city not only to serve the residents of the town but also to nearby areas for their shopping needs and for providing other community facilities and public services. Important district and sub-district centres are:

1. Kunari Sub-District Centre on Bundi Road
2. Umaid Bhawan District Centre
3. Kota Junction
4. Nayapura
5. Old Jall Commercial Area
6. Kansuwa Sub-District Centre
7. Dhakania Talao Station Area
8. Dadabari District Centre
9. Vigyan Nagar Sub-District Centre
10. Chambal Garden Commercial Area
11. Mahaveer Nagar Commercial Area
12. Ladpura
13. Subji Mandi

With the growth of the town, local shopping centres, each having 20 to 25 shops, have sprung up in many residential areas.

Similarly, for day-to-day requirements of the people, convenience or corner shops have been developed in each residential area of the town.

Kota town also has a few well developed wholesale markets. The following table shows the wholesale markets of Kota:

Table 4.3

Wholesale Markets of Kota

1. Grain Markets	(i) New Grain Mandi
	(ii) Old Grain Mandi
	(iii) Umaid Bhawan Area Sabji Mandi
2. Fruits and Vegetable Markets	(i) Sabji Mandi near Tank
	(ii) Near City Railway Station
	(iii) Umaid Bhawan Area
3. Building Materials	(i) Mala Road
	(ii) Near Dhakania Talao railway station
	(iii) Near Water Works
	(iv) Near Sakatpura Grid Station
4. Iron and Steel, Scrap Metal, etc.	(i) Mala Road
	(ii) Near Sophia School
	(iii) Near Dhakania Talao Station
5. Coal and Timber Deports	(i) Mala Road
	(ii) Near Sophia School
	(iii) Near Dhakania Talao Railway Station

There are several small wholesale depots located within the walled city dealing in plastic goods, general merchandise, wood and timber, cloth, furniture (moulded), medicines, etc. There are good storage facilities including warehouses and a cold storage of the government.

As many as 38 banks are functioning in the town. Although Kota has a well developed market system it needs a planned development of markets. A few 'Super Markets' should be developed to fulfil the needs of the growing population.

References

Alam, S.M. (1963), Commercial Structure of the Cities of Hyderabad and Secunderabad, Jr. of Osmania University, Arts, Science, Law and Education (i).

Applebaum, W. (1954), *Marketing Geography in American Geography: Inventory and Prospects*, Syracuse University.

Berry, B.J.L. (1963), Commercial Structure and Commercial Blight, Department of Geography, Research Paper No. 85, University of Chicago.

--- (1965), Metropolitan Planning Guidelines: Commercial Structure, Chicago N. E. Illinois Planning Commission.

--- (1967), *Geography of Market Centres and Retail Distribution*, Prentice Hall.

Cleef, E.V. (1937), *Trade Centres and Trade Routes*, D. Applenton Century Co., New York.

Davies, R.L. (1977), *Marketing Geography*, Methuen.

Gopal Krishan and Agarwal, S.K. (1973), Commercial Pattern of a Planned City: Chandigarh, *National Geographical Journal of India*, XIX.

Mukerjee, R.K. (1968), *Man and His Habitation*, Bombay.

Mulvihill, D.F. and Mulvihill, R.C. (1970), *Geography, Marketing and Urban Growth*, Van Nostrand.

Proudfoot, M.J. (1937), City Retail Structure, *Economic Geography*, Vol. 13, No. 4.

Sami, A. ([illegible]), *Intra-Urban Market Geography*, Concept, New Delhi.

Saxena, H.M. (1978-79), Morphology of Market Towns: Theoretical Aspects and A Case Study of Sriganganagar, *Geographical Outlook*, Vol. 15, pp. 87-93.

— (1990), *Marketing Geography*, Rawat Publications, Jaipur.

Weber, Max (1958), *The City*, The Free Press, Glencoe, Illinois.

Chapter 5

Agricultural Marketing

Agricultural marketing is a process which starts with the decision to produce a farm commodity for commercial purpose involving all aspects of market structure or system, both functional and institutional, through which goods move from producers to consumers. The Indian agricultural marketing system, including that of the Central Hadaoti region has come a long way and is a result of the long play of factors both historical and geographical. Since independence, agricultural production has registered a significant increase, resulting in a large marketable surplus and consequential pressure on the marketing system. With the transformation of agriculture, the marketing pattern has also changed in order to enable farmers to get a price commensurate with the quality of their produce. A vital change in the marketing system has been brought about with the intervention of State machinery in agricultural marketing. Through State action, the market system is geared to achieve the social objectives which cannot be attained by the market mechanism alone. The regulation of agricultural markets has contributed substantially towards increasing the returns to the farmer for his produce and also in systematic development of market yards and other marketing activities. The present chapter aims to discuss the pattern of agricultural marketing in the Central Hadaoti region with special reference to regulated marketing.

Process and Pattern of Agricultural Marketing

Agricultural marketing is a complex phenomenon. It is defined by Thomson (1951: 1) as comprising "all the operations, and the agencies conducting them involved in the movement of farm produced goods, raw materials and their derivatives". The agricultural marketing system is a link between the farm and non-farm sectors. With the development in agricultural sector, the marketing system has also changed. In the Indian context, "agricultural marketing is a process which starts with a decision to produce a saleable farm commodity, and it involves all the aspects of market structure or system, both functional and institutional, based on technical and economic considerations, and includes pre- and post-harvest operation, assembling, grading, storage, transportation and distribution" (XII Report of National Commission on Agriculture).

The functions involved in agricultural marketing are:

(i) Exchange functions
- (a) Buying (assembling)
- (b) Selling

(ii) Physical functions
- (a) Storage
- (b) Transportation
- (c) Processing

(iii) Facilitating functions
- (a) Standardisation
- (b) Financing
- (c) Risk-bearing
- (d) Market intelligence

In fact, marketing functions are activities that are to be performed during marketing of any farm product and all these functions are interlinked with each other, thus forming a part of an efficient marketing system.

Marketing Process

Agricultural marketing as a business activity involves the flow of goods and services from the point of initial production until they reach the ultimate consumer. During this entire process the commodity moves from one hand to another and also from one place to another. But all these actions and events take place in some sequence, which is known as 'marketing process'.

The agricultural marketing process/system starts with the farmer and his production, while at the other end of the system is the consumer. The process starts with movement of farm products to the market and its contact with business firms or traders. The factors affecting this contact are transportation, communication, system of law and order and monetary systems, which are also associated with business management activities. The actual buying and selling activities are done under certain norms and also under some organisational system and ultimately the product first purchased by traders—wholesalers or retailers through middlemen/agents—and reach the consumers. The whole process has been depicted in Fig. 5.1.

Figure 5.1

Generalised Agricultural Marketing Process

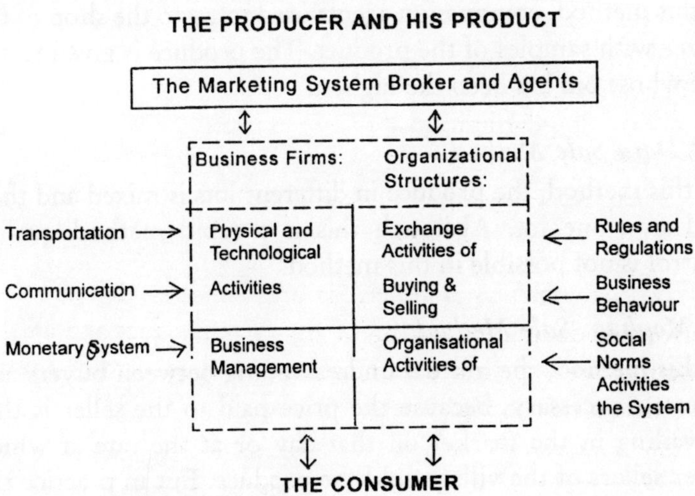

In India, in spite of the existence of regulated marketing, the system of agricultural marketing varies from region to region and also within a region. The prevalent systems are—sale in village, sale in *mandis*, sale in weekly markets, sale of agricultural produce through co-operatives and sales to government. The methods of buying and selling prevalent in Rajasthan including that of region under study are as follows, but most of the systems are not functional today.

(i) Under Cover of a Cloth (Hatha System)

In this system, the prices of the produce are settled by the buyer/commission agent by twisting the fingers under cover of a piece of cloth. The method provides opportunities for cheating the seller as well as the producer. Now this method has been abolished by the government.

(ii) Private Negotiations

The prices of goods are fixed by mutual negotiations, as is common in unregulated markets. In this method the producer farmer is always at the mercy of the traders/agents.

(iii) Quotations on Samples Taken by Commission Agents

In this method, commission agents used to go to the shop of the buyer with samples of the product. The produce is given to the one whose bid has been the highest.

(iv) Dara Sale Method

By this method, the produce in different lots is mixed and then sold as a one lot. Although this is a rapid method quality control is not possible in this method.

(v) Moghum Sale Method

In this method, the mutual understanding between buyers and sellers is necessary, because the price paid to the seller is that prevailing in the market on that day or at the rate at which other sellers of the village sold the produce. But in practice the buyer pays less than the prevailing market rate due to one reason or another.

(vi) Closed Tender System

This is similar to an auction but the rates are not open and bids are invited in the form of a closed tender and the product is given to the highest bidder. This method has also been stopped with the adoption of a regulated marketing system.

(vii) Open Auction Method

The best method of agricultural marketing is the open auction method. Here, the prospective buyers gather at the shop of a commission agent around the heap of the produce, examine it and offer bids loudly. The produce is given to the highest bidder. In regulated markets the auction is done under the supervision of the officials of the market committee. In Central Hadaoti region the open auction system has been adopted according to the Rajasthan State Agricultural Marketing Act, 1961.

The agricultural marketing system of the Central Hadaoti region is similar to that of the rest of the State. The entire process in a generalised form has been depicted in Figure 5.2.

It becomes clear from the figure that two types of marketing system of agricultural products are prevalent in the region, viz., (i) private trade, uncontrolled and without state intervention and (ii) regulated market operations in which trading is done under rules and regulations. In non-regulated markets agricultural products reach the consumer either directly or through a middleman, trader or government agencies. In regulated marketing, an open auction is done by registered traders and agents in the presence of government representatives under specified rules and regulations. Although Rajasthan State has banned systems other than regulated marketing, in unauthorised way, trading of agricultural products has also been done in all parts of the State including

Figure 5.2

Process of Agricultural Marketing

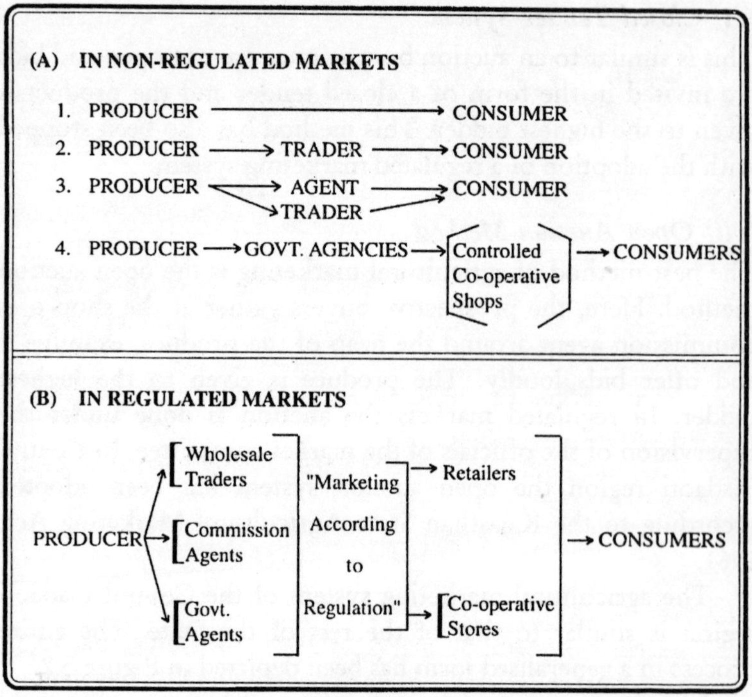

that of the region under study. The regulated system of agricultural marketing system needs a detailed analysis.

Regulated Marketing and Markets

A regulated market is one in which market functionaries are controlled by legislative measures designed to regulate the marketing of agricultural produce. The history of the growth and development of agricultural marketing serves a very useful purpose in knowing the problems of agricultural marketing and their solutions. Prior to the study of the growth of regulated marketing in the region under study, it is necessary to describe in brief its growth in Rajasthan State because the region is an internal part of the State and governed by State rules and regulations.

Growth of Regulated Markets in Rajasthan (including Central Hadaoti)

The present marketing system of agricultural products in Rajasthan is a product of historico-geographical as well as socio-economic conditions prevalent during different periods of history. Although the history of the growth of marketing in Rajasthan is very much similar to that of northern India, it has its own characteristics features too. The growth of regulated markets is a post-independence phenomenon, but its seeds were sown much earlier. For proper analysis of the growth of regulated markets of the State, the entire era can be divided into two broad periods, viz:

(i) Pre-independence period (Ancient and Medieval period), and
(ii) Post-independence period (Modern period).

(i) Pre-independence Period

The earliest system of marketing was no doubt barter, i.e., exchange of commodities. This system is still prevalent in a limited form in the tribal regions of southern and south-eastern Rajasthan including Kota district. What the conditions were of marketing in ancient Rajasthan are still not very clear. But this much is true that periodic marketing as well as trade performed through group of traders known as caravans were common. The non-existence of permanent markets during the ancient period in the State was due to limited demand, limited surplus production and the harsh environmental conditions due to the desert, mountains, forests, etc.

During the medieval period and right through the 17th and 18th centuries till independence, the entire State was divided into several princely States, each having its own administrative system. During this period permanent market centres were developed. State capitals of princely states and towns situated along main routes flourished as business centres or *mandis* such as Pali Nagor, Phalodi, Jodhpur, Bikaner, Bihnmal, Merta, Jaisalmer, Rajgarh, Pugal, Chittorgarh, Udaipur, Bhilwara, Ajmer, Jaipur, Pushkar, Sirohi, Bundi, Kota, Bharatpur, Alwar, Dholpur, etc. State intervention in marketing was also begun in this period to a limited extent. The State Chiefs of Marwar, Mewar, Ambar, Kota, etc., framed rules governing agricultural marketing. In certain cases prices of the products were fixed, some checks had also been imposed on traders to control malpractices in trade and the king used to receive royalty from merchants. Unlike Mughal rulers, the Rajput rulers encouraged trade by providing many facilities and privileges to traders in their states. But they neither monopolised nor engaged themselves in any trade. Their policy was free trade policy, i.e., open to all (Sharma, 1979: 149). In fact, this was the period in which several commercial marts were established and all these markets are now the flourishing trade centres of the State.

This period may be considered as the beginning of State intervention in marketing. That was not a regulated marketing, but some checks and controls were imposed by the State authorities in the form of taxes and supervisory staff had also been appointed. Some taxes prevalent in that period were:

Mapa: it was charged on the goods which were sold in the market, its rates varied from one dhela to one paisa per rupee.

Amad: The tax on goods, which were imported for sale in the market.

Nikasu: This was a tax on goods passing out of a town.

Inchh: This was charged on vegetables, fruits and other edibles brought for sale in the market.

Tulai: This tax was levied on goods which were weighted in the market for sale. It was also known as Kayali in Marwar.

The Britishers exercised their control over all the erstwhile States of Rajasthan, but they too did not take any positive step towards the development of marketing in this region. This was more because at that time the states of Rajputana were not very productive in terms of agricultural production, specially from the British point of view. In brief, prior to independence no efforts have been made to regulate the markets, although centres of agricultural marketing (*mandis*) had been developed in all parts of the region under study.

(ii) Post-independence Period

After independence, the need for regulated markets was felt because the agricultural marketing system was not orderly and various types of malpractices were prevalent in the form of unauthorised deductions such as *dalali*, *dharmada*, *dani*, *muddat*, *kards*, *kabutar*, *chitthi*, *dhalta*, etc., which amounted to about five per cent of total product arrival. By this time several other State governments had already been enacted the Act concerning the establishment of regulated markets. In Rajasthan also the need to regulate the marketing of agricultural products was felt and the first step towards the establishment of regulated markets was taken in year 1956, when the State government created an agricultural marketing organisation in the Department of Agriculture, mainly for market survey and investigations for the establishment of regulated markets. But it became effective only in 1961, when the Rajasthan Agricultural Produce Market Act had enacted with the objective of: (i) providing the producer-seller a remunerative price of his goods, (ii) creating orderly conditions in the market, and (iii) providing consumers with produce of desired standards of quality. After the passing of this Act, detailed rules were framed in 1963 and actual State implementation of the regulation commenced in 1964 with the establishment of regulated markets under the 'Krishi Upaj Mandi Samitis' (Agricultural Produce Mandi Committee) or KUMS. The KUMS is the controlling body of the market, which consists of 15 members, out of which 13 are elected from amongst farmers, traders, local bodies and co-operative institutions. Soon after the establishment of regulated markets in 1964, their number has increased rapidly

Figure 5.3

Central Hadaoti: Regulated Agricultural Markets

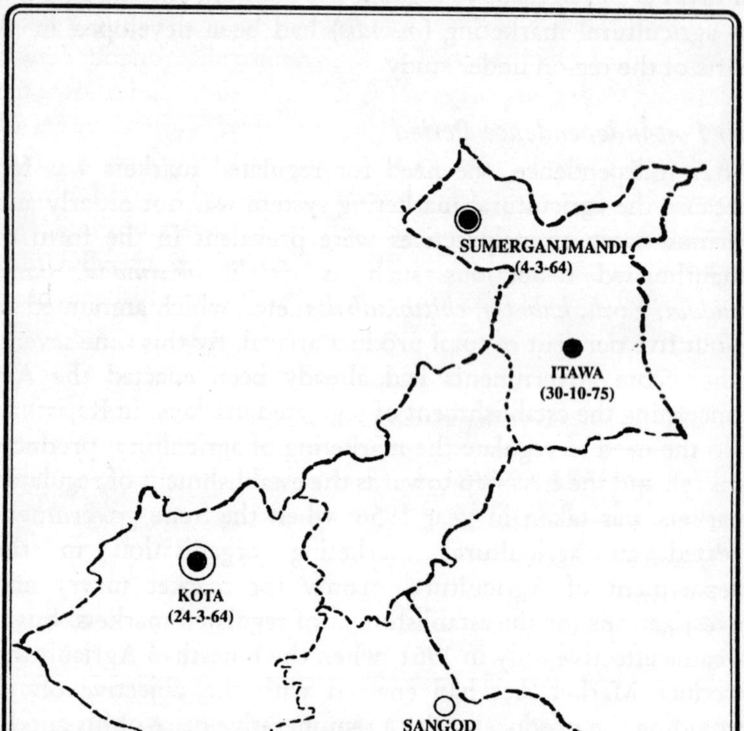

and by the end of 1995, the total number of primary markets and sub-yards in the State was 138 and 240 respectively.

In Central Hadaoti region, the growth of agricultural marketing was similar to that in the rest of the State. As mentioned above Kota has been developed as a leading market centre. Other small towns like Ramganjmandi, Sangod, Itawa, Sultanpur, Chechat, Kanwas, Digod, Pipalda and Indergarh were also developed as collecting and distributing centres of their respective areas. But most of them are very small market centres. With the introduction of the Rajasthan Agricultural Produce Markets Act, 1961, the process of the establishment of regulated markets under Krishi Upaj Mandi Samitis (KUMS) was started and the following regulated markets have been developed (Table 5.1; Fig. 5.3):

Table 5.1

Regulated Markets in Central Hadaoti, 1988

Regulated Market (KUMS)	*Date of Establishment*	*Category*
1. Kota	4.3.64	Super A
2. Sumerganjmandi	4.3.64	B
3. Ramganjmandi	3.5.64	A
4. Itawa	30.10.75	C
5. Sangod	11.11.79	D

It becomes clear from the above table that at present five regulated markets exist in the region. Three of these—Kota, Sumerganjmandi and Ramganjmandi—were established in 1964. No fresh addition was done till 1975 when Itawa was established and the last addition was Sangod, established in 1979. The characteristic feature of the regulated markets of the region is that all the five categories, i.e., Super A, A, B, C and D are present.

Market Yards and Infrastructure

The structural pattern of the agricultural market yard is a significant aspect of geographical study. A market yard or agricultural *mandi* is a place where all marketing activities are performed such as assembling, sale and purchase, grading, storage, banking, etc. This is also a place where all marketing agencies like producer-seller, commission agent, trader, banker, insurance people, administrative agencies, etc., either have their permanent base or they use this place temporarily like farmers. Thus, the market yard is a prominent place of a market town where transactions related to agricultural marketing are performed. Since it is a spatial unit, geographers are interested in their study. Although the layout plan for agricultural markets are prepared by town planners and civil engineers, it is for the geographers to study and suggest the necessary amends in them regarding the infrastructural difficulties and performance evaluation. Only then can further improvements be made. Similarly, the site of the market yard and its relation to the settlement as a whole as well as with market participants' needs, can be done by geographers.

Market Yard Development

One of the objectives of regulated marketing is to establish market yards which are well designed according to the needs of the volume of the business and also for the best interests of the market participants. The need for planned and orderly *mandi* yards has been felt because of difficulties experienced in the previous *mandi* locations (these difficulties are still there in most of the regulated markets, where yards have not been constructed). The following are the common difficulties in traditional or unplanned *mandis*:

(1) The market-place (generally known as 'dhan-mandi' is congested and often located along narrow lanes which do not permit easy access to vehicular traffic. It becomes very difficult for traders to handle their produce and for market committees to supervise transactions.

(2) The shops were often scattered all over the town and the sale and purchase took place all over the locality.
(3) Adequate space was not available for cleaning, grading and exhibiting the produce.
(4) There were no auction platforms. The producer used to sell his produce on the day of its arrival in the market at whatever price.
(5) There was neither space for parking of carts nor for cattle.
(6) Facilities like drinking water, public toilets, veterinary dispensary, canteen, rest house, etc., were not available.
(7) Similarly banks and post offices were located away from *mandis*.

All the above mentioned factors have compelled the marketing authorities in the State to take up a special programme for the development of market yards. Prior to regulation the above mentioned conditions used to exist in all agricultural *mandis*, of the region under study.

After a detailed survey of regulated markets, a report was prepared by the government in 1972-73 for the construction of market yards in the State. Accordingly, in Central Hadaoti region also market yards have been constructed at Kota, Ramganjmandi, Sumerganjmandi and Itawa. Sangod does not have a market yard as yet. At Kota a well-designed market yard was constructed near Chawani Choraha but after 15 years it was realised that this yard has not been able to handle the growing needs of the *mandi* arrivals and there are several other difficulties like location between residential areas, lack of parking facilities, non-availability of space for further construction, etc. Therefore, a new *mandi* has been constructed near Alnia village in 1996-97. A sub-yard at Sultanpur has also been constructed. This is the only sub-yard in the region.

Infrastructure of a Market Yard

A market yard is a place where marketing of agricultural produce is performed and it is also a place where agencies related to agricultural marketing are located. Therefore, from the structural point of view the agricultural market yard is different from other market-places. Every market is supposed to have a standard layout in which there is adequate infrastructural facilities. One of the main objectives of regulated marketing is to construct a planned market yard, where all the facilities are available.

The well designed market yards, beside providing facilities for storage and sale of agricultural produce, etc., also provide facilities for sale of agricultural inputs, banking and insurance. There are also consumer stores where farmers can buy their requirements, a post office, veterinary dispensary, etc. The details of market yard infrastructure are as follows:

(a) Shops-cum-godowns, (b) godowns, (c) retail shops, (d) Market Committee Office including grading laboratory, (e) boundary wall, (f) veterinary dispensary, (f) sale platforms, (g) cattle sheds (h) farmers' guest house, (i) water troughs, (j) water huts, (k) canteen, (i) public urinals, latrines and bath rooms, (m) bank, (n) post office, (o) cycle stand, (p) dust bins (q) chowkidar quarters, (r) internal roads, (s) drainage, (t) water supply arrangements, (u) electricity and lighting arrangements, (v) space for fodder shops, (w) petrol pump, (x) automobile workshop, (y) godowns of FCI, CCI, CWC, etc.

The above mentioned structures/facilities may differ from one market to another in size according to the status of market. With the growth of market the size and number of structures also increase. A brief description of these facilities is necessary for layout planning of a market yard.

1. *Shops*: The general size of shop-cum-godown in Super A, A & B class market is 9x27 m., having auction platform of 9x9m. on the front side, a room of 7x8 m. and godown of 9x7 m. with a space of 3 m. for expansion of godown. Each shop in C class market is of 76x23 m. with an auction platform 6x6 m., a room, 5.5x9 m. and a godown of 7.6x10 m. In front of the shops a *baranda* (gallery) has also been constructed, which is

covered and is used by traders and farmers to store their purchased goods for a short period.

2. *Godowns*: Each A class market will have at least two godowns, each having 250 tonnes capacity, while B and C class market have a provision of one godown of 250 tonnes capacity.

3. *Retail shops*: The suggested number of retail shops in A, B & C class market is 10, 8 and 6 respectively. The size of the shop should be 4x5 m.

4. *Market Committee Office*: The market committee office in A, B and C class market varies in plinth area. It is 300 sq. m. in A class, 260 sq. m. in B class and 200 sq. m. in C class yards. The office comprises of (i) chairman's room, (ii) secretary's room, (iii) general office, (iv) meeting hall and library, (v) publicity room, (vi) rest room, (vii) grading laboratory, and (viii) record room.

5. *Auction platforms*: These platforms are 100 m. long and 7 m. wide with cement flooring. Their size and number vary according to the status of market and also on volume of the agricultural products. In many *mandis* the shade over platform has also been constructed so that products can be saved from heat and rains. These platforms are used for drying, clearing, grading, display and auction of agricultural products.

6. *Rest-house for farmers*: Every planned market yard has a provision for farmers' rest-house depending upon the type of market.

7. *Cattle shed*: In all market yards cattle sheds have been constructed. These are necessary, because most of the farmers bring their products on bullock or camel carts.

8. *Canteen*: For market participants specially for farmers, there is a provision for canteen. The suggested plinth area of canteen for A, B and C class market is 150, 100 and 80 sq. m. respectively.

9. *Other Facilities*: Every planned market yard must have a bank, post office, veterinary dispensary, water hut, cycle stand, public urinals, latrines, bathroom, dust bins, checkpost, chowkidar quarters, etc. The internal roads are generally tarred, and drainage must be provided. The *mandi* committee also provides water and electricity.

In Central Hadaoti region, the Kota Krishi Upaj Mandi is a Super A class *mandi* with a well developed market yard. This yard has been divided into 10 sub-sectors having shops, shops-cum-godowns and an auction platform in front of these shops. The total number of shops and shop-cum-godown is 450, while the number of auction platform is 50. The other facilities available at the Kota *mandi* are well designed market committee office, canteen, farmer's rest house, cattle sheds, bank, post office, water hut, laboratory for quality control, public utility facilities, tarred roads, parking space, etc. The Ramganjmandi yard is also well developed with good facilities for trading and marketing. But market yards of Sumerganjmandi and Itawa are smaller with facilities of marketing according to their lesser status. At Sangod a market yard has not yet been constructed and marketing of agricultural products is being done in the 'dhan-mandi'.

Commodity Structure

The commodity structure of individual regulated agricultural markets and its regional pattern is the product of geographical environment; more the surplus production of agricultural commodities, more will be the regulated agricultural markets. The progress, development, nature and status of a regulated market can be determined by volume and type of commodities passing through the yard for sale and purchase. Generally, all the market towns are having complex commodity structure, but when a market is specialised for a particular commodity or a set of commodities, it attracts a large number of buyers and sellers from widespread areas in comparison to other markets having common commodity structure. The spatial pattern of *mandi* arrivals is a significant aspect of geographical study. Therefore, the study of the commodity structure is one of the most important aspects of the study of regulated markets. This study is not only necessary to understand the present state of agricultural marketing but also of their future planning.

Commodities Under Market Regulation

The Rajasthan Agricultural Produce Markets Act, 1961 has specified the commodities for marketing in regulated markets of the State. The following commodities have been listed after the amendment:

1. Fibres: cotton (ginned and unginned), mesta, jute and semi-hemp.
2. Cereals: wheat, barley, maize, jowar, bajra, paddy and rice.
3. Legumes: moong, urad, arhar, cowpea, peas, gram, groundnut, gowar, kulthi, masoor and moth.
4. Oilseeds: til, sarson, rai, tara-meera, linseed, cottonseed, castorseed.
5. Narcotics: tobacco.
6. Specials: gur, sugar and sugarcane.
7. Fruits: malta, orange, papaya, guava, mango, melon, water-melons, pomegranates, water-chestnuts, banana, ber.
8. Vegetables: potato, sweet-potato, onion, tomato, pumpkin, cauliflower, cabbage, carrot, brinjal, radish, lady's fingers, green chillies.
9. Animal products: egg, poultry, cattle (cow and buffaloes, calves), sheep, goat, milk, butter, ghee, wool, hair, hides and skin.
10. Condiments and spices: zeera, dhania, chillies, methi, fennel, turmeric and ajwain.
11. Fish
12. Forest produce: honey.
13. Miscellaneous: poppy-seed, poppy-husk, mehendi, garden grass and sajji.

Pattern of *Mandi* Arrivals in Central Hadaoti

The present analysis of the arrivals of agricultural products at regulated markets in Rajasthan is based on the data obtained from Rajasthan State Agricultural Marketing Board, Jaipur. The data have been obtained from 1980-81 to 1997-98, i.e., for 18 years. The market-wise data of the arrivals of agricultural commodities has been given in Table 5.2.

Table 5.2

Market-wise Total Arrivals of Agricultural Commodities in Regulated Markets of Central Hadaoti

(*in quintals*)

Years	*Regulated Markets*					
	Kota	*Sumerganj-mandi*	*Ramganj-mandi*	*Itawa*	*Sangod*	*Total of the Region*
1980-81	1365926	55307	222465	165132	44918	1853748
1981-82	077300	76513	240408	24853	57843	1376917
1982-83	842659	69865	342145	21444	41348	1510461
1983-84	2267978	77884	477396	265914	68189	3157361
1984-85	1768370	62815	496164	258089	40630	2992068
1985-86	1927399	57846	509991	229640	629739	3354615
1986-87	2438380	69025	416502	231914	27024	3182845
1987-88	2454727	59572	157984	198135	—	2870418
1988-89	2545108	84346	562000	204090	44505	3440049
1989-90	[illegible]	[illegible]	582796	258795	51842	2562729
1990-91	1602341	83795	623104	273445	53928	2591613
1991-92	963390	—	487150	185310	43770	1679620
1992-93	1658932	84362	598371	282522	54438	2678625
1993-94	1813468	86934	613444	313448	58556	2885850
1994-95	2012115	91389	664892	283014	58996	3110406
1995-96	2038780	125790	716470	254451	61244	3196735
1996-97	1114761	110964	583421	237003	37471	2083620
1997-98	4019833	131405	977683	355028	—	5483949

Source: Rajasthan State Agricultural Marketing Board, Jaipur

Figure 5.4

Trends in Marketwise Arrivals of Agricultural Commodities in Central Hadaoti (1980-81 to 1997-98)

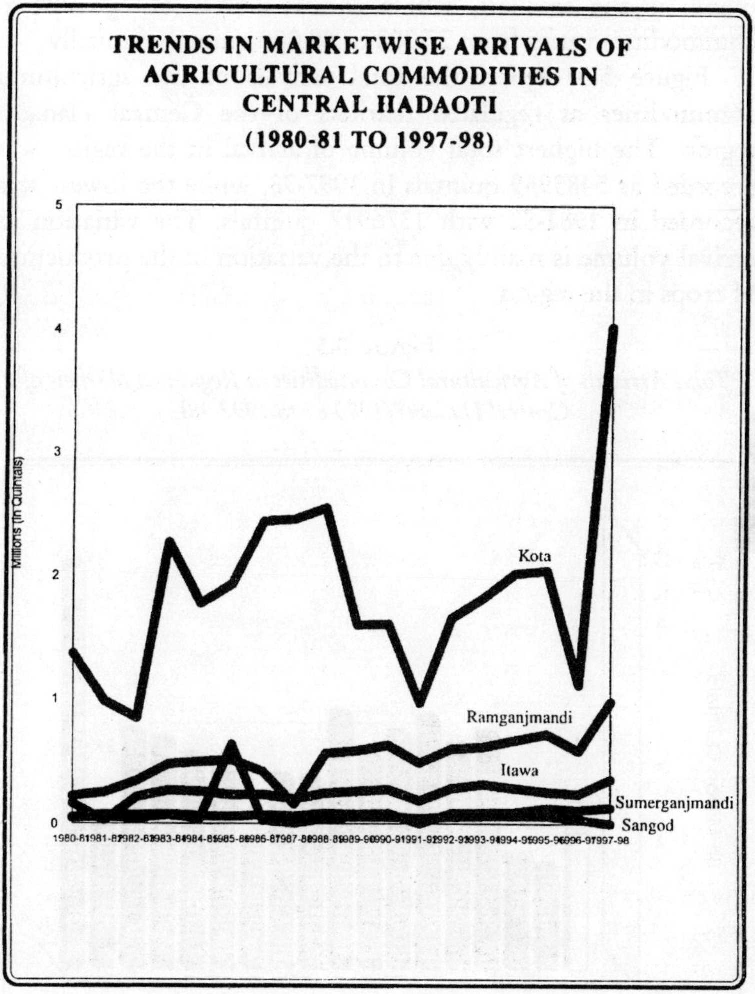

It becomes clear from Table 5.2 and Figure 5.4 that Kota is the leading market in terms of the arrival of agricultural commodities at Krishi Upaj Mandi. The total volume of the arrival at Kota varies from 8 to 40 lakh quintals. Ramganjmandi ranks second in total arrivals with 1.5 to 9.7 lakh quintals. Itawa and Sumerganjmandi rank third and fourth, while Sangod *mandi* is the smallest, where annual arrival of agricultural commodities varies from 27,000 to 68,000 quintals annually.

Figure 5.5 depicts the total arrivals of the agricultural commodities at regulated markets of the Central Hadaoti region. The highest total volume of arrival in the region was recorded as 5483949 quintals in 1997-98, while the lowest was recorded in 1981-82 with 1376917 quintals. The variation in arrival volume is mainly due to the variation in the production of crops in the region.

Figure 5.5

Total Arrivals of Agricultural Commodities in Regulated Markets of Central Hadaoti (1980-81 to 1997-98)

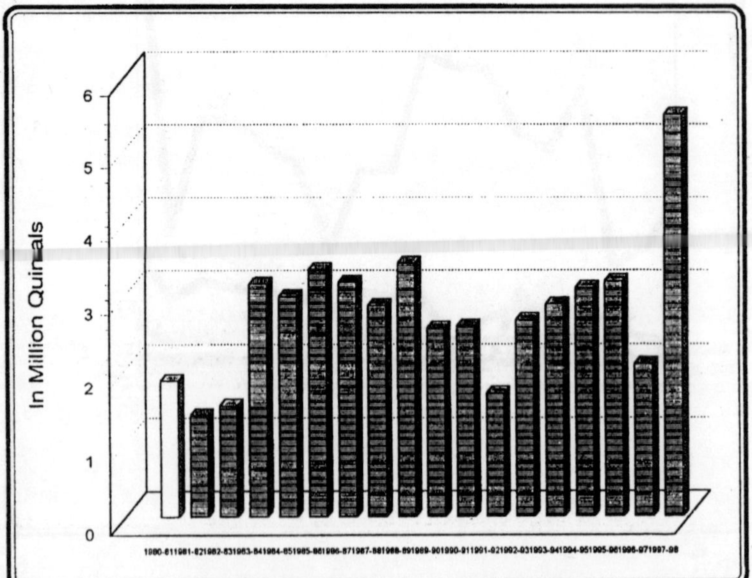

The commodities received for marketing in regulated markets have been categorised as: cereals, pulses, oilseeds, masalas (spices) and others. The following table indicates the category-wise arrival of commodities in Central Hadaoti region.

Table 5.3

Arrivals of Commodities in Regulated Markets of Central Hadaoti (1991-92 to 1997-98)

(*in quintals*)

Year	*Cereals*	*Pulses*	*Oilseeds*	*Masala*	*Others*
1991-92	736300	146860	1023500	504190	50970
1992-93	842964	158293	1182630	452682	42056
1993-94	982131	157382	1018292	302436	38384
1994-95	1027435	131651	1259112	53442	36221
1995-96	1253920	22318	1147951	585963	28321
1996-97	946707	148824	1555627	419678	52989
1997-98	2207534	140370	2525592	585930	31823

Source: Rajasthan State Agricultural Marketing Board, Jaipur.

The above table indicates that oilseeds dominate in agricultural commodities and their arrivals during 1991-92 to 1997-98 varies from 10.2 lakh quintals to 25.2 lakh quintals. The cereals rank second in arrivals with 7.3 lakh to 22 lakh quintals. Pulses and masala (spices) are also important. The region is a good producer to gram, moong, moth, chillies, dhania and methi. A comparison of the category-wise arrivals during 1991-92 to 1997-98 has been shown in Figure 5.6.

Role of Regulated Markets in Development

Regulated markets known as Krishi Upaj Mandis (KUMs) are an integral part of the economic structure and also provide spatial linkages between market towns and their surrounding region. These markets not only provide for sale and purchase facility of agricultural commodities but also help in regional

Figure 5.6

Arrival Pattern of Commodities in Regulated Markets of Central Hadaoti (1991-92 to 1997-98)

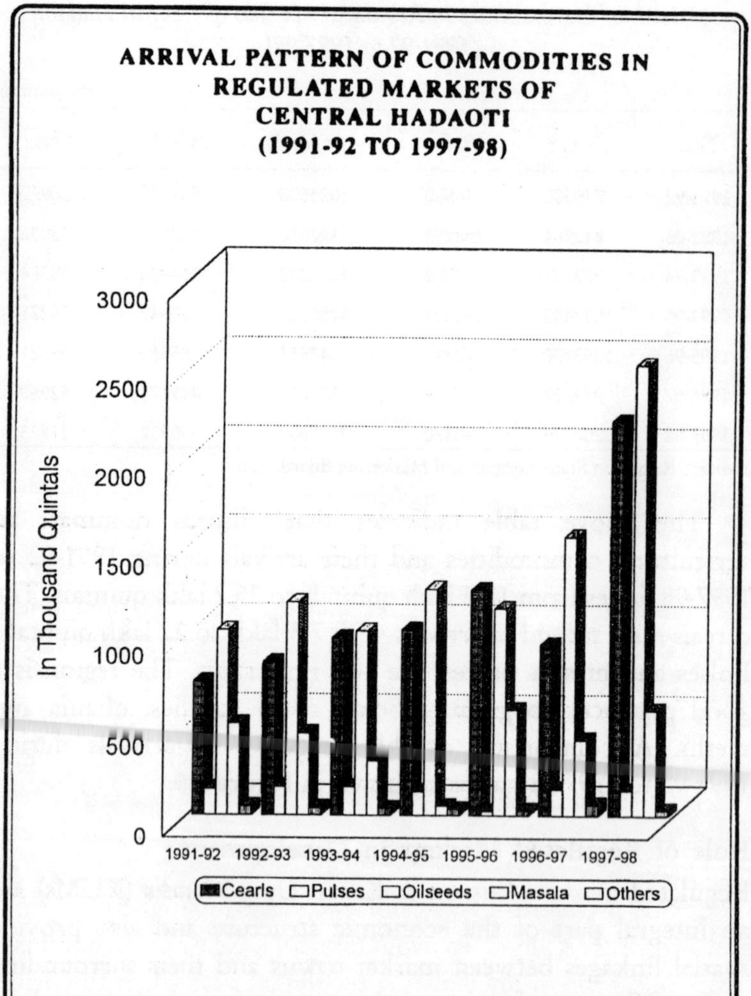

development and rural welfare. They are financially well placed with the income from market fee. The various developmental activities done by KUMS in the region under study are:
(i) development of market yards,
(ii) development of rural markets and rural godowns,
(iii) construction of rural link roads,
(iv) quality control, grading and standardisation, and
(v) rural welfare and regional development.

The development of market yards is the most important work done by market committees with the help of State government and NABARD. The construction of planned and systematic market yards has helped the marketing of agricultural commodities. As described earlier these market yards are having all types of infrastructural facilities according to the category of the market. In Central Hadaoti region, Kota Mandi is having the biggest market yard. In 1995-96 a new market yard has been constructed. Similarly Ramganjmandi, Sumerganjmandi and Itawa are also having market yards. Sangod has not yet developed its own market yard. Apart from the main *mandi*, at Kota, a separate yard for fruits and vegetables has also been constructed.

The development of rural markets has also been done under a new Central Government scheme launched in 1977-78. Under this scheme, a rural market at Sangod has been developed.

Proper storage facility is a prerequisite for the smooth marketing of agricultural products. Storage facilities are more important in rural areas because farmers are not in a position to store their produce even for a few weeks. With this objective in mind a scheme for the establishment of 'National Grid of Rural Godowns' was formulated for creating a network of rural godowns in rural areas to avoid distress in sale and to eliminate losses in storage immediately after the harvest when the prices are low. In these godowns a farmer can hold his stock and can sell his produce as and when prices are high and he can even take loans by placing his produce in such godowns. The State Government has also adopted a scheme to construct rural godowns in 1980-81. In the region under study four rural godowns of 1000 MT capacity and six godowns of 250 MT capacity have been constructed.

The construction of rural link roads is one of the most important development work done by Mandi Committees in the region. These roads have been constructed in order to provide transportation facilities to farmers so that they are able to bring their produce to the market. Their maintenance is also done by the concerned market committee. In Kota district so far 248 kms. link roads have been constructed.

The promotion of grading and standardisation and exercising quality control on agricultural commodities has been one of the principal functions of market regulation. Agmark laboratories have been established at Kota and Ramganjmandi. The grading of agricultural produce is carried out under the provisions of Agricultural Produce (Grading and Marketing) Act, 1973. The grading of agricultural produce is useful not only for consumers but also to traders and producers.

The KUMS also perform several rural welfare activities specially for farmers. Some specific programmes launched in Rajasthan including in the region under study are:

(i) loans to farmers against pledging agriculture produce,
(ii) pay-back of *mandi* fee to small farmers,
(iii) free transportation to small and marginal farmers, and
(iv) assistance for the supply of mini-kits of agricultural inputs to the SC/ST farmers of small and marginal category and marginal farmers from general class.

In general, regulated markets (KUMS) of the Central Hadaoti are doing a good work for rural development. Proper efforts should be made for implementation of welfare schemes so that benefits of above mentioned schemes reach the needy.

References

Sharma, G.C. (1979), *Administrative System of the Rajputs*, Rajesh Publishers, New Delhi.

Thomsen, F.L. (1951), *Agricultural Marketing*, McGraw-Hill.

Chapter 6

Pattern of Rural Marketing

In countries like India, the rural market centres are the farmer's first contact point with the marketing channel. Therefore, rural markets are considered as the nerve-centres of the economic, social and cultural activities of rural life. The producer farmers not only depend on these markets for disposal of their produce for cash, but also for the procurement of agricultural inputs as well as for social contact. The study of the rural market is not only necessary to understand the economic structure of the region but also for unfolding the ecological relationship of the marketing activity. In fact, rural markets are related to regional ecology and are the products of geographical environment. Unlike other forms of marketing, rural marketing is simple but effective and plays a vital role in rural regional economy. The present chapter has been designed to study the characteristic features of the various types of rural markets in the Central Hadaoti region. Prior to actual analysis a brief review of selected works on rural markets is necessary.

Overview of Literature

During the last four decades, there has been remarkable growth of interest among geographers to study rural markets. The volume of literature on rural markets is vast and it is neither possible nor desirable to review the entire literature. For details one must consult the bibliographies prepared by Bromley (1974 and 1979) on 'Periodic Markets, Daily Markets and Fairs'. Two review articles written by R.H.T. Smith (1979, 1980) entitled, 'Periodic Market-Places and Periodic Marketing: Review and Prospects' are notable for their contribution. Another reference to bibliography is the Newsletter No. 15 of the International Geographical Union, a working group on Market Place Exchange Systems, edited by E. Gromsen (1965).

The origin and growth of periodic markets or historical studies have been least attempted by geographers. Hodder (1965) in his paper entitled, 'Some Comments on the Origin of Traditional Markets South of the Sahara' has described the factors responsible for the origin of periodic markets in a part of Africa. Stine (1962) has described the origin of periodic markets as an economic phenomenon. Belshaw (1965) has given a good account of the evolution in marketing systems from traditional exchange to modern markets in various parts of the world. The growth of periodic markets in Singbhum district of Bihar has been discussed by Wanmali (1981).

The periodic market-place, as an element of the spatial system, has been discussed by geographers in the form of spatio-temporal synchronisation, market-place rings and their hierarchies. The relationship between temporal and locational spacing was discussed first by Hodder and Ukwu (1969) and further elaborated by Fagerland and Smith (1970), Smith (1970), Wood (1978), Bromley (1976), Wanmali (1977), etc. They have examined a hypothesis that 'proximity in space implies separation in time' and both direct and inverse relationship has been found in various regions of the developing world. This relationship has also been examined in terms of trader and consumer hypothesis developed and discussed by Smith (1971), Smith and Hay (1969), Gana (1976), Ishihara (1978), Thorpe (1978), Filani and Richard (1976), etc.

Market rings form the base of periodic market network. Such terms as 'ring' (Hodder, 1961), 'cycle' (Thomas, 1924), 'circle' (Polaman, 1961), and 'circuit' (Hill, 1966), have been used and imply the existence of a system. The phenomenon of market cycle has been widely discussed and described by several geographers in various parts of the world including India. The concept of market shift (Alao, 1968) has also been developed in order to explain the system in which the market meetings move from one market to another. The hierarchy of periodic markets has been examined in detail by Skinner (1964), Berry (1967), C.A. Smith (1976) and Bromley (1974). Skinner (1964), in his study of rural China has found that marketing systems exist in an integrated pattern of hierarchy. Several variables like volume of trade, number of shops, total number of people assembled, etc., have been used by geographers in order to study the hierarchical pattern.

Periodicity is an important aspect of rural marketing. In his study of African periodic markets, Good (1973) has suggested that 'the distribution of market periodicities and market networks presents a complex array of functionally, distinct, contiguous, and overlapping systems: a kaleidoscope of place-time interrelationships'. The factor of periodicity has also been examined by Hodder (1971), R.H.T. Smith (1971), Bromley (1975), etc.

In India, considerable research work has been done on weekly markets. Srivastava, Saxena, Tamaskar, Dixit, Wanmali and Gedam have done geographical studies of the various facets of weekly markets. Several Ph.D. theses and research projects have also been completed on periodic markets in the Departments of Geography at Gorakhpur, Udaipur, Sriganganagar, Allahabad, Amrawati, Madurai and Bombay universities.

Another form of rural market in India as well as in other parts of the world is the 'fair'. A number of articles on fairs have appeared in various geographical journals between 1919-1942. As early as 1919, Wrigley's article on "Fairs of Central Andes" was published in *Geographical Review*. In the same journal another notable article entitled, "The Geography of Fairs,

Illustrated by old World Examples", was published by Allix (1922). Fairs in two districts of Madras (Tamil Nadu) have been studied by V. Krishnan (1932,1940). Spencer (1940) has described the Szechwan Village Fair, while Hodgen (1942) has studied the 'Fairs of Elizabethan England', both the papers have been published in *Economic Geography*. Other notable geographical studies of fairs have been done by Kniffen (1949), Hodder and Sinha (1976), Saxena (1972) and Tamaskar (1979).

Types of Rural Markets

In any given region, market centres vary in their nature, size, function and hierarchy. Generally they can be divided into the following types:

(a) Urban and Rural,
(b) Daily and Periodic,
(c) Regulated and Non-regulated,
(d) Wholesale and Retail, and
(e) Local and Regional.

But this classification is effective only for a general description, because a single market, i.e., urban is also daily, regulated, wholesale, retail and regional. Basically, markets are of two types, viz., urban and rural. Among rural markets, the following types have been identified in the Central Hadaoti region:

(a) Periodic Markets
  (i) Weekly and bi-weekly markets, and
  (ii) Fairs
(b) Marketing through mobile traders, and
(c) Permanent village shops and markets.

(a) Periodic Markets

Periodic markets are the characteristic features of rural areas. They function through two institutions, viz., weekly markets and fairs. A weekly market is a weekly assemblage of local traders organised to facilitate retail operations, while a fair occurs occasionally, may be once or twice a year. The total number of weekly markets and fairs in the Central Hadaoti is 25 and 48 respectively.

(b) Mobile Traders

The mobile traders are those salesman who visit rural areas in an individual capacity and on the days they like best with their small goods. Such mobile traders are common throughout the region.

(c) Permanent Village Shops/Markets

There is a misconception regarding rural market that it is only periodic. On the contrary, many villages have permanent markets and a large number of them have shops. All those villages having more than 5000 population have market centres, while others have shops according to the needs of their population.

For a proper understanding of the rural market system a detailed analysis of each type has been done in this chapter.

PERIODIC MARKETS: WEEKLY MARKETS OR *HATS*

In the Central Hadaoti region, as in many other parts of India, the goods and services of daily/permanent market are not available to majority of the rural consumers, because most of the villages are located far from towns. Thus, periodic markets have developed in order to provide opportunities to the rural people to dispose of their farm produce and to satisfy their limited demands.

A periodic market is a public gathering of buyers and sellers of commodities, meeting at an appointed location at regular intervals (Hodder, 1965: 48; Bromley, 1980: 134). The length of market meeting may vary between different cultural areas of the world between one and fourteen days, but in the region under study, such markets are held once in a week. Thus they are known as weekly markets. The per capita demand for goods sold in the market is small, the market area limited by primitive transport technology, and the aggregate demand is therefore insufficient to support permanent shops. Businessmen adjust by visiting several markets on a regular basis; and by accumulating the trade of several market areas they are able to survive (Berry, 1967: 93). In Hadaoti region, as in case of the rest of Rajasthan State, periodic (weekly markets) are locally known as *hat* or *hatwara* and are the nerve centres of the economic, social and cultural activities of the people.

Distribution of Weekly Markets

In Central Hadaoti, weekly markets are distributed throughout the region. In all, there are 25 centres where weekly markets are held. The following table (Table 6.1) indicates tehsil-wise, the number of weekly markets in the region.

It becomes clear from table and Figure 6.1 that Piplod and Ramganjmandi tehsils are having seven and six centres respectively, where weekly markets are held, followed by Digod and Sangod tehsils with five and four centres respectively. In Ladpura tehsil only three centres have weekly markets. It may be presumed that the existence of Kota town is the reason but this is not true because at Kota also a weekly market is held every Sunday. The existence of more weekly markets in south-western and north-eastern parts of the region is due to the dissected topography and scattered distribution of villages rather than any other economic reason.

Periodic or weekly markets are not only a spatial phenomenon but they also have a temporal aspect. This time-space relationship has been referred to as 'spatio-temporal synchronisation' by geographers. The hypothesis 'proximity in space implies separation in time' (Fagerland and Smith, 1970: 343) and trader-consumer hypothesis (Hill and Smith, 1972: 345-53) not only explain the space-time relationship but also the nature and utility of periodic markets in the modern economic context.

Table 6.1

Tehsil-wise Distribution of Weekly Markets in Central Hadaoti

Tehsil	*Centres/Places*	*Market Day*	*Total Number of Weekly Markets in Tehsil*
Piplod	Jana	Tuesday	
	Bamori Kaln	Monday	
	Itawa	Thursday	
	Indergarh	Sunday	7
	Gantia	Sunday	
	Piplod	Saturday	
	Sumerganj Mandi	Saturday	
Digod	Barod	Tuesday	
	Badoti	Sunday	
	Rel	Saturday	5
	Digod	Sunday	
	Sultanpur	Thursday	
Ladpura	Kota	Sunday	
	Bamani	Monday	3
	Mandana	Thursday	
Sangod	Awan	Monday	
	Kanwas	Wednesday	4
	Sangod	Monday	
	Dhulet	Tuesday	
Ramganjmandi	Chechat	Friday	
	Ramganj Mandi	Tuesday	
	Morak	Monday	6
	Khairabad	Saturday	
	Suket	Saturday	
	Dara	Sunday	
	Total		25

The analysis of a spatio-temporal relationship of weekly markets in the region has been examined with the help of distances occurring on same day, adjacent day, one day and two

Figure 6.1
Distribution and Schedule of Weekly Markets in Central Hadaoti

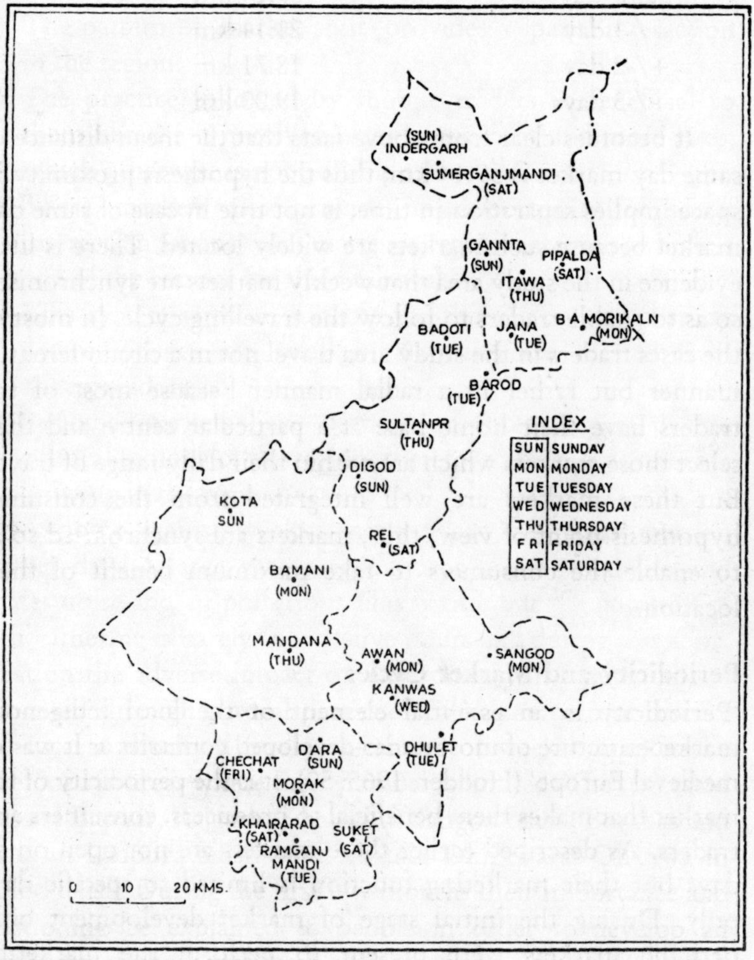

days' interval. The analysis reveals the following facts for Central Hadaoti region.

Temporal and Locational Spacing of Weekly Markets
(Mean distance between the market)

Same day	39.14 km
+/-1 day	21.14 km
+/-2 day	18.71 km
+/-3 days	19.00 km

It becomes clear from above facts that the mean distance of same day market is 39.14 km, thus the hypothesis proximity in space implies separation in time, is not true in case of same day market because such markets are widely located. There is little evidence in the study area that weekly markets are synchronised so as to enable traders to follow the travelling cycle. In most of the cases traders in the study area travel not in a circumferential manner but rather in a radial manner because most of the traders have their home base at a particular centre and they select those markets which are within their daily range of travel. But these markets are well integrated from the consumer hypothesis point of view, thus, markets are synchronised so as to enable the consumers to take maximum benefit of their location.

Periodicity and Market Cycles

'Periodicity is an essential element of the local indigenous market-structure of most under-developed countries as it was of medieval Europe' (Hodder, 1965: 50). It is the periodicity of the market that makes them beneficial to producers, consumers and traders. As described earlier these markets are not open on all days but their marketing function is limited to specific days only. During the initial stage of market development only periodic markets were present to perform the marketing function, but in due course of time permanent shops/markets developed and at present in many centres both permanent and weekly markets are found side by side. The occurrence of periodic markets on some specific day is a special feature of many rural regions. As Good (1972: 211) has observed, marketing calendars regulate the frequency of a market and define the length of the 'market week' for a given area and its set of markets. These calendars frequently have a pervasive influence on many other aspects of economic and social life. The system of periodicity provides an adjustment with the agricultural system. Only one marketing day in a seven-day-week means six rest days or days of other agricultural activity and rural folk get sufficient time for relaxation as well as for preparation for the next visit to the market.

In Central Hadaoti, all the periodic markets are held once in a week, and are therefore termed 'weekly markets'. In other words these markets have a weekly periodicity. Although weekly markets locally known as *hatwara* may be held on all the days of the week, Sunday is the most popular day when the market is held at six centres. This is followed by Monday and Saturday when it is held at five places on each day. On Wednesday only one weekly market is held at Kanwas. The schedule of market days is given in Table 6.2.

Periodic markets in a region are interlinked in a system which controls the movement of traders as well as consumers in some cases and is known as the 'market cycle'. The term market cycle denotes the regularity in movement of goods and people between producer and the consumer In Rajasthan State, a well developed system of market cycle exists as described by Saxena (1988: 42-45) but since the region under study is a small unit (Kota district only), well developed market cycles are not common. However, in some case the sequential movement of traders has been traced as shown in Figure 6.2. It becomes clear from the figure that three-day market cycles between (i) Awan (Monday), Dhulet (Tuesday) and Kanwas (Wednesday) exist in Sangod Tehsil; (ii) Sangod, (Monday), Dhulet (Tuesday) and Kanwas (Wednesday) also in Sangod tehsil; and (iii) Suket (Saturday), Dara (Sunday) and Morkak (Monday) in Ramanganjmandi. The two-day sequence is a common feature.

Table 6.2

Schedule of Market Days in Central Hadaoti

Market Day	*Places*	*Number*
1. Sunday	1. Indergarh	
	2. Gantia	
	3. Digod	6
	4. Kota	
	5. Dara	
	6. Badoti	
2. Monday	1. Bamori Kaln	
	2. Bamni	
	3. Awan	5
	4. Sangod	
	5. Morak	
3. Tuesday	1. Jana	
	2. Baroda	4
	3. Dhulet	
	4. Ramganjmandi	
4. Wednesday	1. Kanwas	
5. Thursday	1. Itawa	
	2. Sultanpur	3
	3. Mandana	
6. Friday	1. Chechet	
7. Saturday	1. Piplod	
	2. Sumerganjmandi	
	3. Rel	5
	4. Khairabad	
	5. Suket	
Total		25

Other markets are isolated. Some of the markets of the region which are located at the border of adjacent districts are interlinked with markets located in other districts also.

Figure 6.2
Central Hadaoti: Market Cycles in Weekly Markets

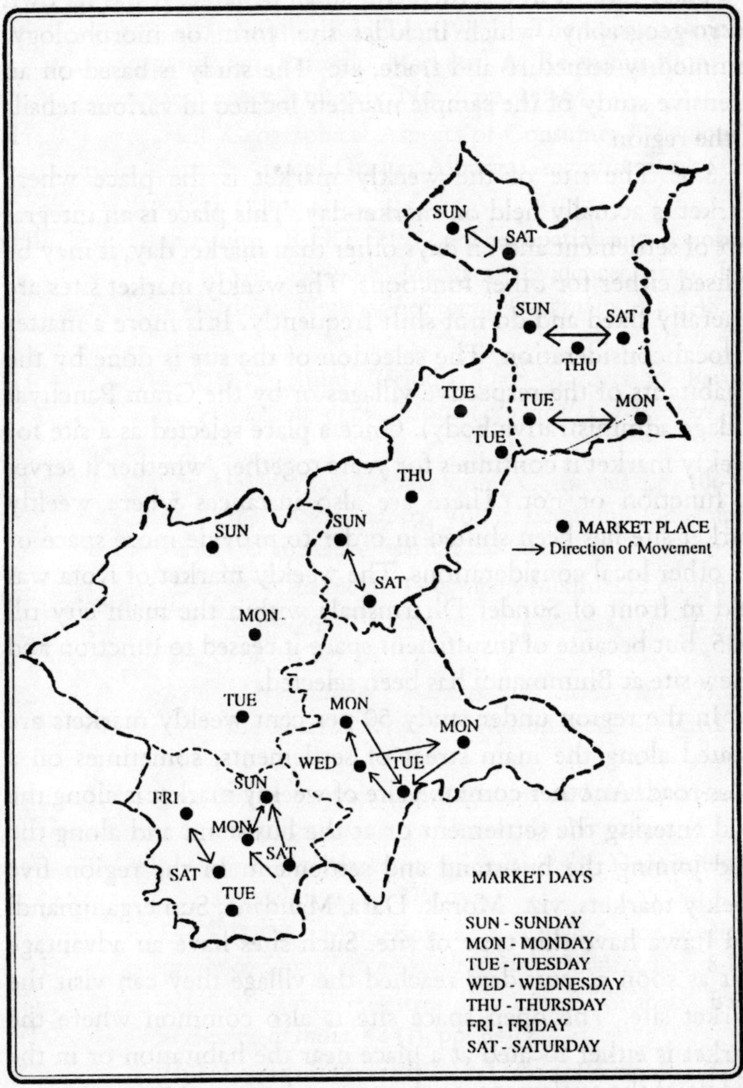

Internal Organisation of Weekly Markets

The internal organisation of weekly markets is a result of geographical conditions since every weekly market has its base at a place located in a settlement, small or large. It has its own micro-geography, which includes site, form or morphology, commodity structure and trade, etc. The study is based on an intensive study of the sample markets located in various tehsils of the region.

Site: The site of the weekly market is the place where market is actually held on market-day. This place is an integral part of settlement and on days other than market day, it may be utilised either for other functions. The weekly market sites are generally fixed and do not shift frequently. It is more a matter of local consideration. The selection of the site is done by the inhabitants of the respective villages or by the Gram Panchyat (village administrative body). Once a place selected as a site for weekly market it continues for years together, whether it serves its function or not. There are also instances where weekly market site has been shifted in order to provide more space or for other local considerations. The weekly market of Kota was held in front of Sunder Dharmshala within the main city till 1955, but because of insufficient space it ceased to function and a new site at Bhimmandi has been selected.

In the region under study 50 per cent weekly markets are located along the main street of settlements, sometimes on a cross-road. Another common site of weekly market is along the road entering the settlement or at the bus-stand and along the road joining the bus-stand and settlement. In the region five weekly markets, viz., Morak, Dara, Mandana, Sumerganjmandi and Itawa have this type of site. Such sites have an advantage that as soon as outsiders reached the village they can visit the market site. The open space site is also common where the market is either located at a place near the habitation or in the middle of the settlement. Such sites can be seen at three markets in the region. Sometimes the weekly market is held either around the temple or the village panchayat house, or a place specially designed for this purpose.

In general, the selection of the weekly market-site in Central Hadaoti is governed by one or more of the following factors:

(i) proximity to the existing permanent market, if any;
(ii) proximity to roads or road joining the settlement with other settlements in the neighbourhood; and
(iii) proximity to a common meeting ground like a temple, 'panchayat', or an open space in the centre of the habitation.

Morphology

The weekly markets are superimposed structures although they are an essential part of a settlement. The structures (shops) arranged for markets are temporary, and sometimes there may not even the any structure at all. The sellers sit along the road itself without any shade. Even then weekly markets have a morphological pattern which is governed by street pattern and/or arrangement of shops. In weekly markets arrangement of shops is orderly, sections are earmarked and most of the traders have their fixed places. There is also a fair level of specilisation in these markets. Generally, similar type of shops such as vegetables, cloth, general merchants, etc., are located together, so that consumers may compare goods and their prices and make a fair choice of the required goods.

The layout of the weekly markets of Suket, Dara, Sumerganjmandi and Kota have been depicted in Figure 6.3. The arrangement of shops determine the entire plan of the market. The main street of the village or town is a determining factor as in case of Dara and Sumerganjmandi while the weekly market of Suket is held around the temple located at the main *choraha* of the habitation. At Kota, the space along station road near Manoj Cinema is used for this purpose. Generally, similar

Figure 6.3
Layout and Shop Pattern in Sample Weekly Markets

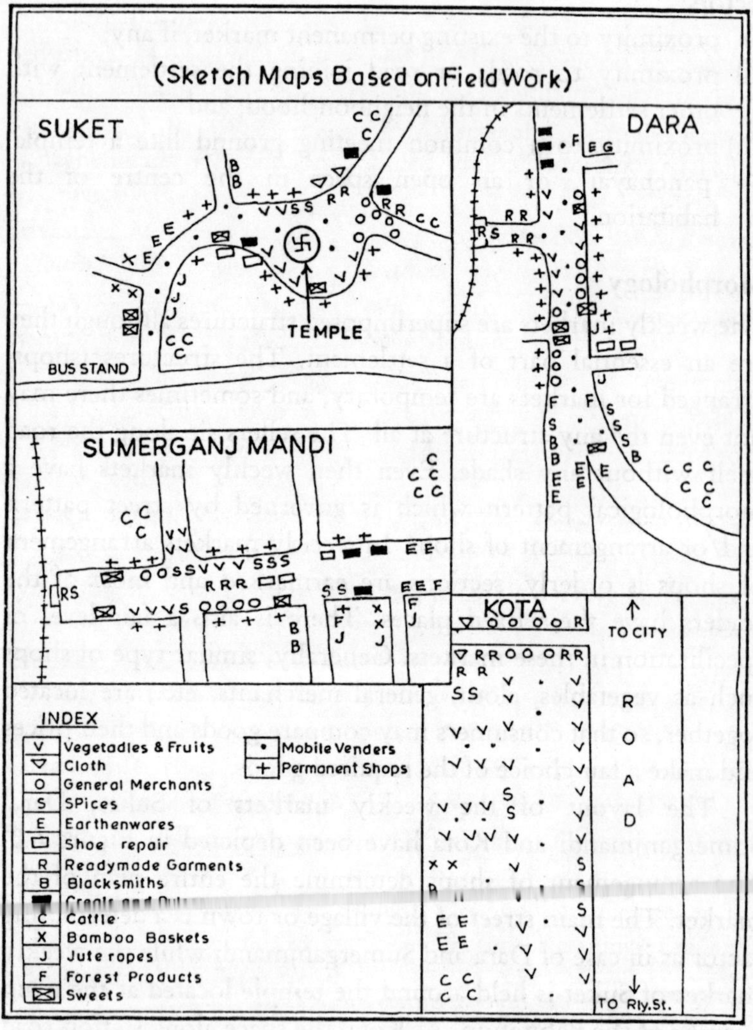

type of shops have been arranged side by side and most of the shopkeepers have their shops at fixed places on every market day.

Commodity Structure

The weekly markets are a place for sale and purchase of different types of commodities. On the basis of a survey conducted in the region under study a general classification of commodities in weekly markets has been done in the following manner:

Commodity Structure of Weekly Markets in Central Hadaoti

1. Agricultural Products
   (i) Vegetables and fruits
   (ii) Foodgrains, pulses and oilseeds
   (iii) Chillies, dhania, tobacco
2. Animals and Animal Products
   (i) Animal
   (ii) Hides
   (iii) Ghee
3. Other Food Articles
   (i) Oil: mustard, groundnut and til
   (ii) Gur
   (iii) Sweets
   (iv) Salt
   (iv) Spices
4. Forest Products
   (i) Firewood
   (ii) Mahua
   (iii) Other products
5. Handicraft Products
   (i) Earthenware
   (ii) Bamboo baskets
   (iii) Shoes

(iv) Handloom cloth
(v) Smith products
(vi) Indigenous agricultural implements

6. Manufactured goods
   (i) Millmade cloth
   (ii) Readymade garments
   (iii) Hosiery articles
   (iv) Fancy goods
   (v) Soaps
   (vi) Plastic goods
   (vii) Kerosene oil
   (viii) Aluminium ware, etc.
7. Service shops of barbers, carpenters, blacksmiths, cycle repair, lock repair, shoe repair, etc.

MARKETING PROCESS

The marketing process in weekly markets is common throughout the State, including the region under study. Basically, the marketing system in these markets is simple and direct. Profit is the primary motive of both traders and consumers, therefore, there is much haggling in prices and one can see a lot of variation in prices of the same products in early and late hours of marketing on market day and at times in different shops at the same time. The marketing process as studied in sample markets has been depicted in Figure 6.4.

The Figure indicates the direct marketing process in which producers and traders engage themselves on market days. Sometimes, the producer goes to the trader for sale, and at other times the trader goes to the producer to purchase his goods and then resells it in the market. In places, middleman are also involved between producers and consumers collecting a commission from both parties.

The entire marketing system in operation in all the weekly markets in the region under study is shown in Figure 6.4 III. In this system the producer contacts the consumer in the

Figure 6.4

Marketing Process in Weekly Markets

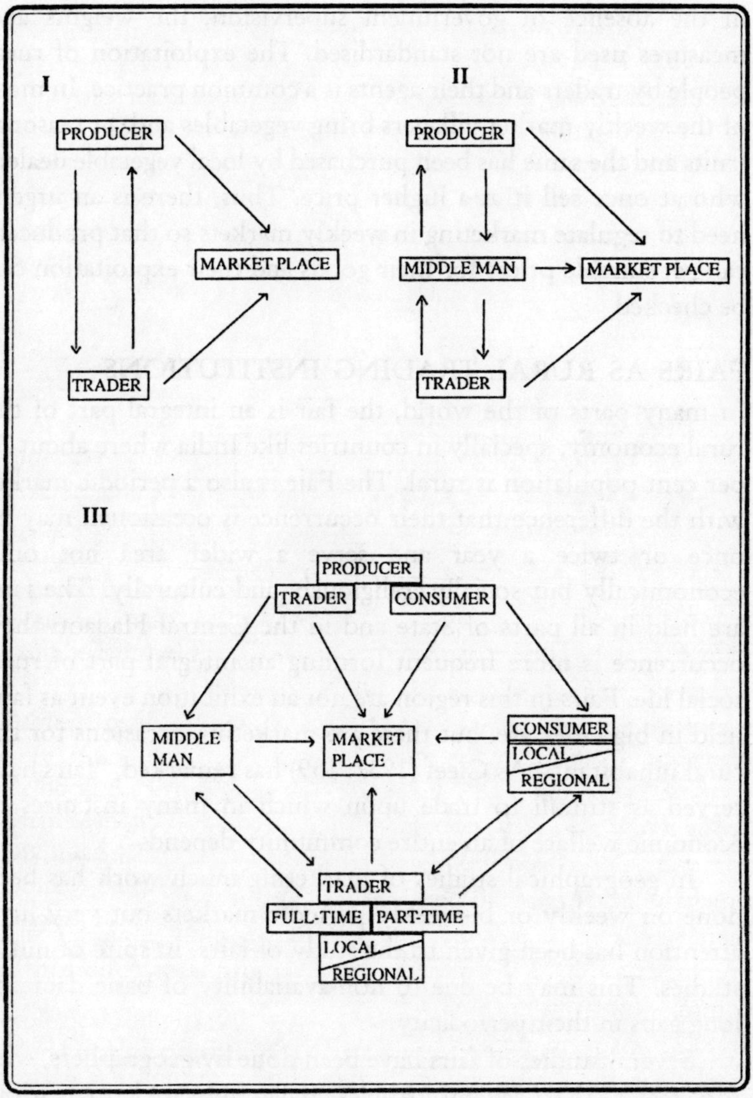

market-place or he goes to the trader through a middleman. The middleman, trader, consumers and of course producers meet at market-place, settle terms and conditions and purchase and sell the goods. The whole marketing system is still traditional, and in the absence of government supervision, the weights and measures used are not standardised. The exploitation of rural people by traders and their agents is a common practice. In most of the weekly market villagers bring vegetables and/or seasonal fruits and the same has been purchased by local vegetable dealers who at once sell it at a higher price. Thus, there is an urgent need to regulate marketing in weekly markets so that producers can get suitable prices for their goods and their exploitation can be checked.

FAIRS AS RURAL TRADING INSTITUTIONS

In many parts of the world, the fair is an integral part of the rural economy, specially in countries like India where about 75 per cent population is rural. The Fair is also a periodic market with the difference that their occurrence is occasional, may be once or twice a year and serve a wider area not only economically but socially, religiously and culturally. The fairs are held in all parts of State and in the Central Hadaoti their occurrence is more frequent forming an integral part of rural social life. Fairs in this region are not an exhibition event as fairs held in big cities are, but these are marketing occasions for the rural inhabitants. As Cleef (1937: 139) has remarked, "fairs have served as stimuli to trade upon which in many instances of economic welfare of an entire community depends".

In geographical studies of marketing much work has been done on weekly or bi-weekly periodic markets but very little attention has been given to the study of fairs, in spite of initial studies. This may be due to non-availability of basic data and long gaps in their periodicity.

Several studies of fairs have been done by geographers, with the result that several articles have appeared in various geographical journals between 1919 and 1942. Of these, the papers of Wrigley (1919), Allix (1922), Krishnan (1932, 1933), Kendall (1934), Spencer (1940), Hodgen (1942) and Deshpande (1942) are notable. Their studies are related to the fairs of Central Andes, India, France, China, England, etc. These studies also provide a base for a geographical study of fairs and unfold the characteristic features of fairs in various parts of the world. While discussing 'Trade Centres and Trade Routes' Cleef (1937: 139-144) has described fairs as trading institutions. Kniffen (1949, 1951) in his study of the American agricultural fair, finds that it is closely related to the ancient harvest festival. Saxena (1972) has presented a detailed geographical account of the fairs of Rajasthan (1988: 74-95). The 'Fairs Around Calcutta' have been described by Hodder and Sinha, while Tamaskar (1979) has presented a detailed account of the fair centres of the Chhattisgarh Plain.

"Fairs rank among the oldest as well as the most fascinating of trading institutions" (Cleef, 1937: 139). The origin of fairs goes back to remote times. In the ancient world annual fairs were held at natural sites, in or near temples at the time of some religious festival and under the protection of local chiefs. Fairs also came into existence at places where merchant caravans had to halt to change their means of transportation, or where multitudes of people assembled at particular times for a religious festival. In fact, the term 'fair' is derived from the Latin word *feariae* meaning feast.

In Rajasthan, including the region under study, the fair seems to be an ancient trading institution. Their initial growth was in the form of social gathering at the time of religious festival or at some holy place. But soon exchange of commodities and trade in small quantities were started in order to fulfil the needs of the people of the limited area. Since it was a social-cum-religious-cum-commercial gathering it was successful and became popular among the masses. Thus, every princely

Figure 6.5

Central Hadaoti: Location and Distribution of Fairs

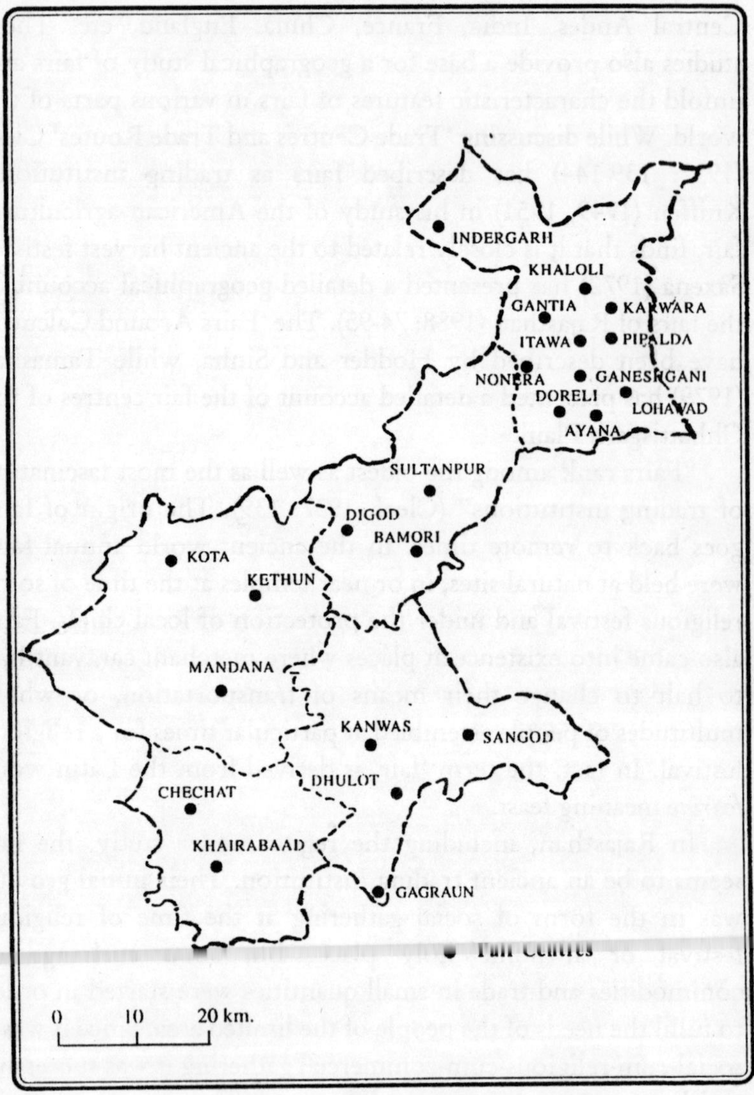

State and their zamidars issued orders for fairs in order to promote trade links with other states and also to provide local traders a good market for their goods. They also granted several concessions and incentives for participation in these fairs, specially to outside traders. Thus, in the medieval period, fairs were a popular feature and still continue to perform the same function throughout the State.

The old records of Kota clearly indicate the occurrence of fairs in which local and foreign traders participated. Realising the importance of fairs the rulers considered the organisation of fairs as their duty. The Hakim of the *pargana* in whose jurisdiction the fair was going to be held was to go in person to arrange for the safety of traders and their merchandise. He also made arrangements for fodder or grass and water. A police station or *kotwali chabootra* was also established in the fair where armed persons were kept ready to provide necessary protection to traders and other participants. All the fairs in the region have been started during the pre-independence period to act as rural trading as well as social institutions.

Distribution of Fairs

Fairs are held throughout the region. But their occurrence is more in Pipalda tehsil where 26 out of the total 48 fairs are held. The tehsil-wise number of fairs has been given in the following table:

Table 6.3

Tehsil-wise Number of Fairs in Central Hadaoti

	Tehsil	*No. of Fairs*
1.	Ladpura	04
2.	Ramganjmandi	03
3.	Sangod	06
4.	Digod	09
5.	Pipalda	26
	Total	48

The distribution of fairs with place names, dates and approximate number of participants has been given in Table 6.4.

Table 6.4

Fairs of Central Hadaoti Region

	Place	*Name of the Fair*	*Dates*	*No. of days*	*Total partici-pants*	*Category*	*Tehsil*
1.	Kota	Dashera	Ashvin Sudi5 to Kartik Bandi 15	11	500,000	Commercial	Ladpura
2.	Kaithoon	Cattle Fair	Every Thursday	01	1,500	Commercial	Ladpura
3.	Mandona	Cattle Fair	April	02	800	Commercial	Ladpura
4.	Umedganj	Donkey Fair	Kartik Sudi 15	15	5,000	Commercial	Ladpura
5.	Chechat	Tejaji	Bhadrapad 10	01	2,000	Religious	Ramganj-mandi
6.	Chechat	Narsinghdeoji	Vaishak Sudi 3	02	5,000	Commercial	Ramganj-mandi
7.	Khairabad	Phalodi Mata	Magh Sudi 5	02	15,000	Religious	Ramganj-mandi
8.	Kanwas	Ramnavami	Chaitra Sudi 9	01	5,000	Religious	Sangod
9.	Dhoolet	Ramnavami	Chaitra Sudi 9	01	5,000	Religious	Sangod
10.	Gujariya heri	Dudhiya Kheri Mata	Magh Sudi 7	02	10,000	Religious	Sangod
11.	Gagron	Mithe Sahib	Before Moharrum	04	15.000	Religious	Sangod
12.	Sangod	Cattle Fair	Jaistha Sudi 1 to 10	11	35,000	Commercial	Sangod
13.	Sangod	Nahan	Chaitra Bedi 3 to 7	05	15,000	Entertainment	Sangod
14.	Chauma Mallyan	Shivratri	Phalgun Badi 14	01	3,500	Religious	Digod
15.	Bamori	Moti Maharaj	Aug.-Sept.	01	1,200	Religious	Digod
16.	Sultanpur	Baba Ratiyaji	February	01	2,500	Religious	Digod

Contd...

Contd...

17.	Sultanpur	Tejaji	Bhadrapad 10	01	2,000	Religious	Digod
18.	Digod	Tajaji	Bhadrapad 10	01	1,500	Religious	Digod
19.	Padaliya	Tejaji	Bhadrapad 10	01	1,200	Religious	Digod
20.	Kadsawan	Tejaji	Bhadrapad 10	01	2,000	Religious	Digod
21.	Doongarja	Tejaji	Bhadrapad 10	01	10,000	Religious	Digod
22.	Sultanpur	Cattle Fair	Asadh Bhadrapad	03	4,500	Commercial	Digod
23.	Hari Pura	Shivratri	Phalgun Badi 14	01	2,500	Religious Pipalda	Pipalda
24.	Nonera	Shivratri	Phalgun Badi 14	01	3,000	Religious	Pipalda
25.	Gondi	Shivratri	Phalgun Badi 14	01	1,500	Religious	Pipalda
26.	Itawa	Tejaji	Bhadrapad Sudi 10	01	5,500	Religious	Pipalda
27.	Luawad	Tejaji	Bhadrapad Sudi 10	01	1,800	Religious	Pipalda
28.	Ganeshganj	Tejaji	Bhadrapad Sudi 10	01	800	Religious	Itawa
29.	Baroli	Tejaji	Bhadrapad Sudi 10	01	500	Religious	Itawa
30.	Itawa	Mahaveer Jayanti	Chaitra Sudi 14	01	6,000	Religious	Itawa
31.	Itawa	Dashura	Ashvin Sudi 10	01	4,000	Religious	Itawa
32.	Binayka	Dashera	Ashvin Sudi 10	01	3,500	Religious	Itawa
33.	Luawad	Dashera	Ashvin Sudi 10	01	4,500	Religious	Itawa
34.	Itawa	Moharrum	10th of Moharrum	01	5,000	Religious	Itawa
35.	Ayana	Akshya Tritiya	Vaishak Sudi 3	01	10,000	Religious	Itawa
36.	Dorli	Pobuji	Kartik Sudi 4	01	2,500	Religious	Itawa
37.	Indergarh	Kawaleshwar Mahadev	Kartik Sudi 15	03	15,000	Religions & Comm.	Pipalda

Contd...

Contd...

38.	Indergarh	Gopreshwar Mahadev	Margshirsh Badi 2	04	2,800	Religious & Comm.	Pipalda
39.	Indergarh	Mataji	Vaishak Sudi 15	02	10,000	Religious	Pipalda
40.	Phoosod	Mataji	Magh Budi 2-6	05	22,000	Religious & Comm.	Pipalda
41.	Pipalda Kalan	Tejaji	Bhadrapad Sudi 10	01	5,000	Religious & Comm.	Pipalda
42.	Karwar	Tejaji	Bhadrapad Sudi 10	01	8,000	Religious & Comm.	Pipalda
43.	Telab	Tejaji	Bhadrapad Sudi 10	01	3,500	Religious	Pipalda
44.	Karwar	Shivratri	Phalgun Badi 14	01	2,000	Religious	Pipalda
45.	Kakrala	Shivratri	Phalgun Budi 13	08	25,000	Religious & Comm.	Pipalda
46.	Khatoli	Ganesh Chaturthi	Bhadra pada Sudi 4	01	5,000	Religious	Pipalda
47.	Geta	Basant Panchmi	Magh Sudi 5	01	5,000	Commercial	Pipalda
48.	Khatoli	Cattle Fair	Every Thursday of Ashvin Sudi	01	3,000	Commercial	Pipalda

Periodicity and Schedule

Periodicity is the most important aspect of fairs. The importance of a fair can be judged from the number of days it lasts. If the length of a fair is long it will attract more persons from a wider area and in turn more will be the volume of trade. The following table indicates the periodicity of the fairs held in the region.

It becomes clear from Table 6.5 that out of the total of 48 fairs, 33, i.e., 68.5 per cent are one-day fairs associated with some religious festivals. A special Donkey Fair is held for 15 days at Umedganj followed by Dashera fairs of Kota of 11 days duration. Other fairs have a two to eight days' periodicity.

Table 6.5
Periodicity of the Fairs in Central Hadaoti

Periodicity (Number of days)	*Total Number of Fairs*
One day	33
Two days	05
Three days	02
Four days	02
Five days	02
Eight days	01
Eleven days	02
Fifteen days	01

Another aspect of the study of fairs is their schedule, i.e., dates on which fairs are held. There is a marked seasonal variation in the occurrence of fairs in the region. The monthly variation has been given in Table 6.6 and Figure 6.6.

Table 6.6
Monthly Variation in Fair Schedule

Name of the Month (According to Hindu calendar)	*Total No. of Fairs*
Chaitra	04
Vaishak	02
Jaistha	01
Ashad	01
Shrawan	Nil
Bhadrapad	14
Ashvin	05
Kartik	04
Margshirsh	01
Paush	Nil
Magh	03
Phalgun	06

Since the date of the fair is fixed according to Hindu months, the same has been taken as the base for Table 6.6. Two

Figure 6.6
(a) Periodicity of Fairs in Central Hadaoti
(b) Monthly Variation in Fair Schedule

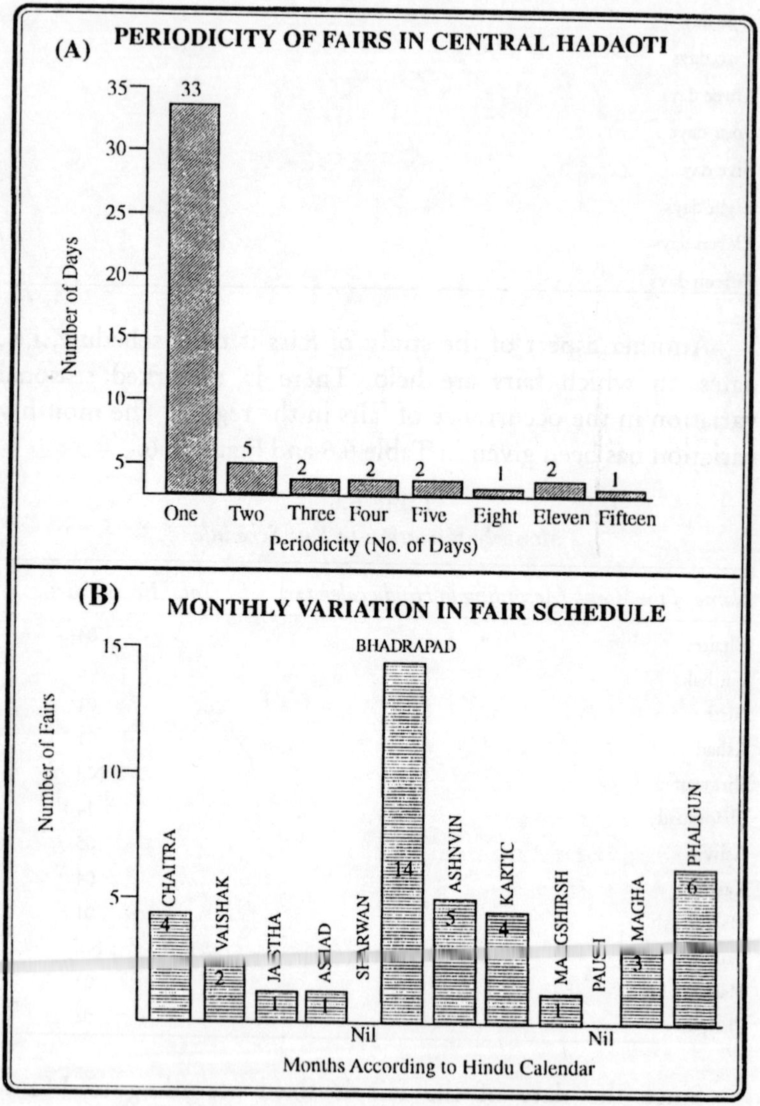

Muslim fairs (*Urs*) are also held in the region and their dates are based on the Islamic calendar. The table reveals that Bhadrapad (September) is the most popular month in which 16 fairs are held in the region. This month is actually at the end of the rainy season. Similarly in Phalgun (March) six fairs are held followed by five in Ashvin. In Shrawan (July) and Paush (January) not a single fair is held due to the rains and peak winter.

Types of Fairs

According to Saxena (1988: 79-80) the fairs of the Central Hadaoti can be classified into the following types:

(A) On the basis of their primary purpose
- (i) Religious fair
- (ii) Commercial fair
    - (a) Commodity fair
    - (b) Cattle fair
    - (c) Commodity-cum-cattle fair
    - (d) Exhibition fair
    - (e) Mixed fair

(B) On the basis of their periodicity
- (i) One day fair
- (ii) Short duration fair
- (iii) Long duration fair

(C) On the basis of their importance
- (i) Local fair
- (ii) Regional fair
- (iii) Inter-region fair

For the present analysis fairs have been classified into the following categories:

(i) Religious fair
(ii) Religious-cum-commercial fair
(iii) Cattle fair

(i) *Religious Fairs*: Most of the fairs in the region under study have taken their origin in religion or religious motives. This is because religion is a very strong motivating force in

Indian culture and has capability to attract people. Most of the fairs are held either on festival days or at some holy place like temple or tomb. In the region 12 fairs are associated with Tejaji (local god having control on snakes). All these fairs are held on 10 Sudi of Bhadrapad. Nine fairs are held on Shivratri. Fairs are also held on Dashera, Ramnavami, Vasant Panchmi or at temples of Devi Mata, Mahadev, Hanumanji. One Muslim fair is held at Gagron at the tomb of Mithe Sahib and another at Itawa on 10th of Moharrum.

(ii) *Religious-cum-Commercial Fairs*: In this category, those fairs have been included which are religious in origin but commercial activities are also performed. Generally, when people gather at any place, some commercial activity is also done. Sometimes it is in the form of a few stalls, while in other cases well organised shops have been arranged. About 50 per cent fairs of the region can be included in this category, but more specifically 17 fairs are in the category of religious-cum-commercial.

(iii) *Cattle Fairs*: Cattle fairs are more common not only in the Central Hadaoti but in whole of the State. In these fairs sale and purchase of cattle is done on a large scale. In the region eight cattle fairs are held. A unique cattle fair is held at Umedganj of Ladpura tehsil in which only Donkeys are brought for sale and purchase. This fairs continues for 15 days and attracts traders and purchasers not only from Rajasthan but also from MP, Maharashtra, Gujarat. Other cattle fairs are held at Kota (Dashera fair), Kaithoon, Sangod, Sultanpur and Khatoli.

Marketing in Fairs

A fair also acts as a rural marketing institute. It originated as a place where marketing could be performed during the fair period. Fairs have always been social and economic institutions but in modern times they also play a vital role in the rural economy.

The number of shops in a fair varies from 10 to 500 depending upon their importance and periodicity. In one-day fairs most of the shops are related with sweets (*prasad*) and items for children. In religious-cum-commercial fairs many types of shop are arranged in a systematic manner. In rural fairs of the region following type of shops are common: sweets, *namkin* and tea, *manihari*, grocery, general merchandise, cigarettes and *pan-biri*, bamboo sticks, hair cutting, photo-studio, cloth, shoes, medicines, musical instruments, earthen pots, religious books and photos, brassware, knife, coconut and ghee, hides, blankets and bedsheets, wooden items, agricultural implements, readymade garments, smithy products, fashionable items for ladies, cinema, circus, etc. In cattle fairs, cattle are scattered in the periphery zone of the fair. These are centres of entertainment and exhibitions arranged by various State departments as well as by private companies. The Dashera fair of Kota is the largest fair not only of the region but also of the State. This is a planned fair having permanent shop structures. The Dashera fair of Kota attracts traders and other participants not only from adjoining districts of Bundi, Baran, Jhalawar, Tonk and Sawai Madhopur, but also from many parts of the rest of Rajasthan as well as from Madhya Pradesh, Delhi and Punjab.

Other Agencies of Rural Marketing

In Central Hadaoti two other forms of rural marketing agencies exist, i.e., village shops and mobile traders.

Village Shops or Permanent Market-places

The study of rural marketing in the region reveals that in many villages, permanent shops also exist. Their number, nature and size varies according to the population of the village. In fact, all the villages having population of 1,000 or more have permanent shops. In villages where population is less than 1,000 the number of shops are less than five, dealing *kirana*, sweets, tea stalls, *pan-biri*, etc. In Kota district there are 219 villages having more than 1000 population in 1991.

The villages shops are located along the main street of the village and near the bus stand. A few shops are also scattered in other areas. Most of these shops are also the part of the residence. In the region under study six villages are having more than 5,000 population. In these villages the number of shops varies from 35 to 56. The following types of shop can be seen in the village market---grocer (*kirana* or *parchun*), cloth, general merchants, tea-stalls, sweets, tailor, cycle repair, shoes, barber, carpenter, medicine, stationery, foodgrains, etc. In fact, these village shops are rudimentary markets and represent the initial stage of development of the market.

Mobile Traders

Mobile traders are those merchants who move from one village to another, from one house to another in order to sell commodities which are often required by rural folk. In this pattern of marketing a shop comes to the customer through mobile traders. These travelling salesmen serve the remote villages which are not having any marketing facility, periodic or daily. The prime reason for the existence of mobile shops as stated by Stine (1962: 68) that when the maximum range is smaller than the threshold requirement of the firm (market), the firm either ceases to function or else it becomes mobile.

Mobile traders are common in the Central Hadaoti region. The daily number of mobile traders moving out from sample towns by their own vehicles are as shown in Table 6.7.

The movement pattern of mobile traders depends upon their capacity. Generally, they follow a definite route and try to visit four to five villages in a day. Most of the traders use the cycle as a mode of transport. All the mobile traders have their home base in towns. The most common practice in mobile traders in the region is that they move from door to door with their merchandise. While moving from one house to another

Table 6.7

Daily Number of Mobile Traders using their own Vehicles

(based on one week average)

S.No.	*Name of the Town*	*Tehsil*	*No. of Mobile Traders*
1.	Sangod	Sangod	58
2.	Ramganjmandi	Ramganjmandi	120
3.	Digod	Digod	42
4.	Itawa	Piplod	36
5.	Sumerganjmandi	Piplod	32

they used to announce loudly the name of the commodity they sell, such as *kapada* (cloth), *chadar* (bedsheets), *khilona* (toys), *churi* (bangles), etc. The prices are not fixed and there is considerable haggling. The payment is made either in cash or in kind in the form of foodgrains. Some mobile traders also display their goods at some vantage point in the village. The popular goods sold by them are general merchandise, readymade garments, cloth and fancy items for ladies. In brief, mobile traders serve the rural people in a very modest form. But they are an integral part of the rural marketing system.

References

Alao, N.A. (1962), Periodic Markets in Western Nigeria: Theory and Empirical Evidence, Northeastern University, Department of Geography, Research Report 42.

Allix, A. (1922). The Geography of Fairs: Illustrated by Old World Examples, *Geographical Review*, Vol. 12, pp. 532-69.

Berry, B.J.L. (1967), *Geography of Market Centres and Retail Distribution*, Prentice-Hall.

Bromley, R.J. (1974), Periodic Markets, Daily Markets and Fairs: A Bibliography, *Monash Publication in Geography No. 10 and A*

Bibliography Supplement to 1979, Centre for Development Studies, Swansea.

---- (1975), Marketing and Central Place Systems in Less Developed Countries, *Area*, Vol. 7, No. 2. pp. 125-26.

--- (1976), Contemporary Market Periodicity in Highland Ecuador, in Smith, C.A. (ed.), *Regional Analysis*, Vol. I. Academic Press, New York.

Cleef, E.V. (1937), *Trade Centres and Trade Routes*, D. Application Century Co., New York.

Davies, R.L. (1976), *Marketing Geography*, Methuen, London.

Fagerland, V.G. and Smith R.H.T. (1970), A Preliminary Map of Market Periodicities in Ghana, *Journal of Developing Areas*, 4, pp. 334-47.

Gana, J.A. (1976), The Locational Pattern and Functions of Periodic Markets in Zaria Division, Nigeria, *Savanna*, 1963-74.

Garnier, B.J. and Delobez, A. (1979), *Geography of Marketing*, Longman, London.

Good, C.M. (1973), Markets in Africa: A Review of Research Themes and the Question of Market Origins, *Cahiers D'Etudes Africaines*, 13, pp. 769-80.

Gromsen, E. (1885), Market Place Research, Newsletter No. 15, Geographisches Institute Der Johannes Gutenberg University, Mainz.

Hodgen, M.R. (1942), Fair of Elizabethan England, *Economic Geography*, 18, pp. 389-400.

Hodder, B.W. (1961), Rural Periodic Day Market in Part of Yorubaland, *Transactions of the Institute of British Geographers*, No. 29, pp. 149-59.

---- (1965), Some Comments on the Origins of Traditional Markets in Africa South of Sahara, *Transactions of the Institute of British Geographers*, No. 36, pp. 97-105.

---- and Ukwu, U.I. (1969), *Markets in West Africa*, University of Ibadan Press.

---- (1971), Periodic and Daily Market in West Africa, in Meillassous, C. (ed.), *The Development of Indigeneous Trade and Markets in West Africa*, Oxford.

---- and Sinha, R.M. (1976), Fairs Around Calcutta, *Geographical Review of India*, Vol. 38, pp. 187-92.

Hill, P. (1966), Notes of Traditional Market Authority and Market Periodicity in West Africa, *Journal of African History*, 7, pp. 295-311.

Ishihara, H. (1978), A Study on the Temporal and Spatial Arrangement of Periodical Markets, Journal of the Faculty of Literature of Nagoya University, 74, pp. 169-85.

Kendall, H.M. (1936), Fairs and Markets in the Department of Gers, France, *Economic Geography*, Vol. 12, pp. 351-358.

Kniffen, F. (1949), The American Agricultural Fair: Time and Place, *Annals of the Association of American Geographers*, Vol. 39, pp. 264-79 and 1951, Vol. 41, pp. 42-57.

Krishnan, V. (1932), Fairs and Trade Centres of Madras and Ramnad Districts, *Journal of the Madras Geographers Association*, Vol., 7, No. 3, pp. 237-49.

---- (1940), Fairs, Festivals and Shandies in Trichy District, *Journal of Madras Geographers Association*, Vol. 15, No. 3, pp. 272-76.

Saxena, H.M. (1984), *Geography of Marketing*, Sterling, New Delhi.

— (1988), *Rural Markets and Development*, Rawat Publications, Jaipur.

Scott, Peter (1970), *Geography and Retailing*, Hutchinson, London.

Smith, R.H.T. (1970), A Note on Periodic Markets in West Africa, *African Urban Notes*, Vol. 5, No. 2, pp. 29-37.

---- and Hay (1969), A Theory of Spatial Structure of Internal Trade in Under-Developed Countries, *Geographical Analysis*, Vol. 1, pp. 121-36.

---- (1971), West African Market Places: Temporal Periodicity and Locational Spacing, in Meillassoux C. (ed.), *The Development of Indigenous Trade and Markets in West Africa*, Oxford, London.

---- (1979), Periodic Market-Place and Periodic Marketing: Review and Prospects-l, *Progress in Human Geography*, Vol. 3, No. 4, pp. 473-505 and 1980, Vol. 4, No. 1, pp. 1-31.

Smith, C.A. (1976), Markets in Oxaca: Are they Really Unique?, *Readings in Anthropology*, 3, pp. 386-400.

Skinner, G.W. (1964), Marketing and Social Structure in Rural China, Pt. l, *Journal of Asian Studies*, 24, pp. 3-43.

Stine, J.H. (1962), Temporal Aspects of Tertiary Production Elements in Korea, in Pitts P.R. (ed.), *Urban Systems and Economic Development*, Engene, Oregon.

Spencer, J.E. (1940), The Szechwan Village Fair, *Economic Geography*, Vol. 16, pp. 48-58.

Tamaskar, B.G. (1979), The Fair-Centres of the Chhattisgarh Plain, *The National Geographer*, 14, 1.

Wanmali, S. (1981), *Periodic Markets and Rural Development in India*, B.R. Publishing Corporation, Delhi.

Wood, L.J. (1978), Rural Markets in Kenya, in Smith, R.H.T. (ed.), *Market Place Trade*, University of British Columbia, Vancouver.

Wrigley, G.M. (1919), Fairs of the Central Andes, *Geographical Review*, Vol. 7, pp. 65-80.

Chapter 7

Behavioural Pattern of Market-Place Participants

The behavioural pattern is an important but complex phenomenon in marketing which, although varying from individual to individual forms a guiding principle of development planning. Geographers have only just begun to search the surface as far as their understanding of the detailed composition of the behaviour of market participant is concerned. The new approach of study is known as 'cognitive behavioural approach', which is a systematic framework, starting with the individual decision-maker as the basic unit of analysis. The individual's behaviour is viewed as a function of the environmental situation and the decision-making process with respect to the environment (Downs, 1970).

Marketing not only involves linkages between inter-settlement and territorial units but also interaction among various individuals and/or groups of the society associated with marketing activities. A significant proportion of human energy is spent in acts of exchange such as sale of farm produce, sale of non-farm produce, purchase of farm and non-farm inputs and purchase of consumable goods. Over time the acts of exchange have continually increased in their magnitude and complexities. The behavioural pattern of market participants is a key component, which directs and determines the growth of market centres and also reflects the functioning of the space economy. The behavioural pattern of market participants is an important aspect of research which can be explained by knowing (i) where people go for marketing, (ii) what are their preferences, (iii) what is the difference in movement pattern for various purposes of marketing, (iv) whether these differences are due to socio-economic considerations or otherwise, etc. The factors which control the preferences in the choice of market-places may vary from status and standard of a person to his or her perception to relative location, accessibility, infrastructural facilities, etc. There are also several other considerations which require intensive study.

Key Questions and Hypotheses

The key questions and hypotheses selected for the present study are as follows:

(1) that consumers will always visit the nearest shopping centre that offers required goods or services;

(2) that the range of consumers' needs increases with the increase in specialisation of a centre;

(3) that all shopping trips are multi-functional in nature;

(4) that more the accessibility more will be the market participants;

(5) that more the specialisation more will be the marketing activities;

(6) that market regulation is more beneficial to farmers than traders/agents;

(7) that markets are synchronised so as to enable the traders to follow the routes which minimise their weekly travel cost (trader hypothesis, Smith, 1971);

(8) that markets are synchronised so as to enable the consumers to have easiest possible access to market throughout the week (consumer hypothesis, Smith, 1971); and

(9) that behavioural pattern of market participants is an outcome of:
   (a) locational convenience
   (b) merchandise suitability
   (c) price
   (d) store services
   (e) congeniality
   (f) post-purchase satisfaction.

Market-Place Participants

Marketing is a system through which goods and commodities move from producer to consumer, thus it is the participants who make marketing an effective function. Although there is some difference of participants in various systems of marketing, in every marketing system there are common participants such as producers, traders, middleman and consumers. The following participants/agencies play a controlling role in marketing.

Producers: Farmers, industrialists, mine owners, artisans, livestock owners, etc., are all included in the category of producer. Any product produced needs its channel so as to reach the hands of consumers. There are small producers, who visit market themselves with their produce and sell it either to the trader/agent or to the consumer. Such producer-sellers are common in periodic markets. On the other hand, there are big producers and company owners having a big and complex chain of marketing. Whatever may be his status the fact is that producers are the cornerstones of marketing activity, and they may participate directly or indirectly in marketing activity.

Traders: Merchants or traders are those individuals who buy and sell goods on their own and gain or lose, depending on the difference in the sale and purchase prices. Two common types of traders are wholesalers and retailers.

Wholesalers: Wholesalers are those merchants who buy and sell commodities in large quantities. They may buy either directly from the producers or through an agency or a middleman. They sell to retailers, other wholesalers and processors but they do not sell to the ultimate consumers. The wholesalers perform functions like: (i) assembling the goods from various agencies, (ii) sorting out goods according to quality and brands, (iii) controlling the flow of goods according to demands, (iv) providing finance to producers, and (v) assessing the demand of prospective consumers and providing information to respective producers. Thus, they control the market mechanism.

Retailers: Retailers buy goods from wholesalers and sell them to the consumers in small quantities. Retailers are the closest to the consumers in the marketing channel. Itinerant traders and village merchants who move from village to village also come under this group. In periodic markets mobile merchants move from one market to another along with their merchandise, while in towns retailers have their fixed shops.

Middlemen: Middlemen are those individuals or business concerns who specialise in performing the various marketing functions and rendering such services as are involved in the marketing of goods. They do this at different stages in the marketing process. Their role in agricultural marketing is more important because they provide a link between producer and seller. They serve as buyers or sellers in effective bargaining and receive their commission or brokerage. Therefore, they are known as commission agents or *Arhatias*. Apart from agricultural marketing, middlemen play an important role in other forms of marketing including periodic marketing.

Consumers: The ultimate objective of marketing is to provide required items to the consumers. In fact, the marketing function end only with consumer. The role of a consumer is vital and controlling. The behavioural pattern of the consumers determine the entire nature of marketing, its growth and future possibilities. This is more important in urban marketing but its importance cannot be denied in rural and periodic marketing.

Other Participants: Other participants in the marketing activity are *hammals* or labourers, weightmen, graders, transport agencies, advertising agencies, banking and insurance agencies, etc. The market officials and officials working in trading institutions like State Trading Corporation (STC), FCI, NAFED, Co-operatives, etc., have had their own role in marketing.

In brief, each market-place participant performs his function and is an important link in marketing mechanism. Effective marketing requires complete co-ordination among market participants. The present analysis deals with behavioural patterns of market-place participants in urban and rural or periodic markets. The study is based on field work conducted at two urban centres, viz., Kota and Ramganjmandi and eight periodic markets.

Consumer Behaviour in Urban Markets

The whole structure of the urban markets is determined by consumer behaviour and its study is a new field in geography. Davies (1976: 227) has rightly observed that "The subject of consumer behaviour is an extremely complicated one and geographers have really only just begun to search the surface as their understanding of the detailed composition of individual shopping trips is concerned". But geographers have studied the various aspects of consumer behaviour, and as Stimson (1987: 163) stated, "Consumer behaviour has traditionally been a fertile area of research in geography. Because of the inherent spatial nature of consumer shopping activity—where the consumer is likely to shop directly affects the location and organisation of the retail market system and vice-versa".

The present study is based on data collected from primary sources, i.e., directly from the consumers. The survey has been conducted in two towns—Kota and Ramganjmandi. Kota is the biggest urban centre and ranks third among the urban centres of the State, while Ramganjmandi represents a medium sized traditional market centre of the region. On the basis of the collected data, conclusions have been drawn in terms of hypothesis mentioned earlier.

The Pattern of Consumer Behaviour

Choice of Shopping Centres

Whether consumers always visit the nearest shopping centre for his required goods—this hypothesis has been examined on 300 respondents and the results are as follows:

Table 7.1

Consumers' Choice of Shopping Centres (in terms of distance)

Category	*Kota*		*Ramganjmandi*	
	No. of Respondents	*Percentage*	*No. of Respondents*	*Percentage*
Nearest centre	24	12	22	22
Main markets	58	29	38	38
Other centres located in between	76	38	32	32
Specialised markets	42	21	08	08

It becomes clear from the above table that consumer preference is more for main markets and markets located between the main market and the nearest centre. At Kota 38 per cent consumers visit markets located in between. This is because at Kota residential areas are located in a widespread areas and several clusters of shops/shopping centres have been developed. At Ramganjmandi the main market is popular followed by in between market centre. The percentage of preference for nearest centre is 12 and 22 respectively at Kota and Ramganjmandi. On the other hand, 21 per cent consumers at Kota visit specialised markets, this percentage is only 08 at Ramganjmandi. Thus, the hypothesis that consumers always visit a nearest centre is partially true.

Shopping Trip Frequency

The shopping trips have been performed according to needs and convenience. The number of shopping trips performed per week in two market towns has been given in Table 7.2.

Table 7.2
Frequency of Weekly Shopping Trips

Category	*At Kota*		*At Ramganjmandi*	
	No. of Respondents	*Percentage*	*No. of Respondents*	*Percentage*
Once a week	92	46	24	24
Twice a week	38	19	17	17
Thrice a week	21	10.5	18	18
Four days in a week	17	8.5	16	16
Daily	32	16	25	25

It becomes clear from the above table that 46 and 24 per cent consumers go to the shops only once a week for their purchases at Kota and Ramganjmandi. On the other hand, the percentage of daily visitors is 16 and 25 at Kota and Ramganjmandi respectively. The twice, thrice and four times a week frequency varies between 8 and 19 per cent. The shopping trip frequency varies with income. The persons engaged on daily wages basis purchase goods of their necessity daily.

Mode of Travel

The mode of travel used for shopping has its direct impact on distance travelled as well as on trip frequency. The various modes of transport adopted by consumers in the region are as follows:

Table 7.3 indicates that maximum shopping is done on foot, its percentage has been recorded as 67 and 58 at Kota and Ramganjmandi respectively. This is followed by the cycle and power driven two wheelers. In fact, most of the population is in the lower and middle income group. In many cases, families having power driven vehicles also prefer going for shopping on foot.

Figure 7.1

Urban Consumer's Choice of Shopping Centres

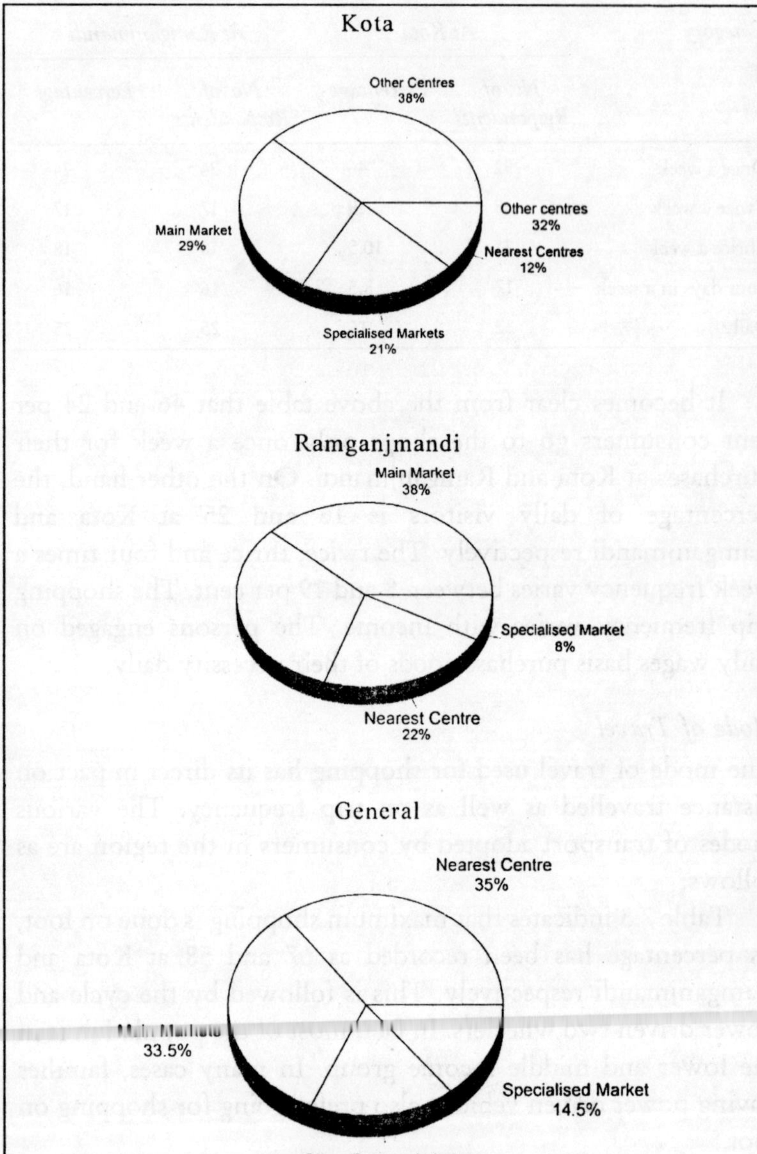

Table 7.3
Mode of Travel Used for Shopping

Category	*Kota*		*Ramganjmandi*	
	No. of Respondents	*%*	*No. of Respondents*	*%*
On Foot	134	67	58	58
Cycle	34	17	26	26
Scooter/Motorcycle	22	11	15	15,
Car	10	5	01	01

Purpose of Market Trips

Table 7.4 indicates the purpose of market trips:

Table 7.4
Purpose of Market Trips

Category	*Kota*		*Ramganjmandi*	
	No. of Respondents	*%*	*No. of Respondent*	*%*
Only purchase	34	17	28	28
Purchase on way to working place	68	34	30	30
Multi-purpose	98	49	42	42

It becomes clear from the above table that most of the market trips are multi-purpose in nature. People go to the market for various services, during their visit to neighbours and relatives or simply as a routine. About 30 to 34 per cent consumers make their purchases while returning home from their working place. Only 17 per cent consumers at Kota and 28 per cent at Ramganjmandi have specific purpose of purchasing a particular item. In most of the cases this type of trip has been performed either to purchase vegetables or some specific durable goods.

Figure 7.2
Urban Consumer's Frequency of Weekly Shopping Trips

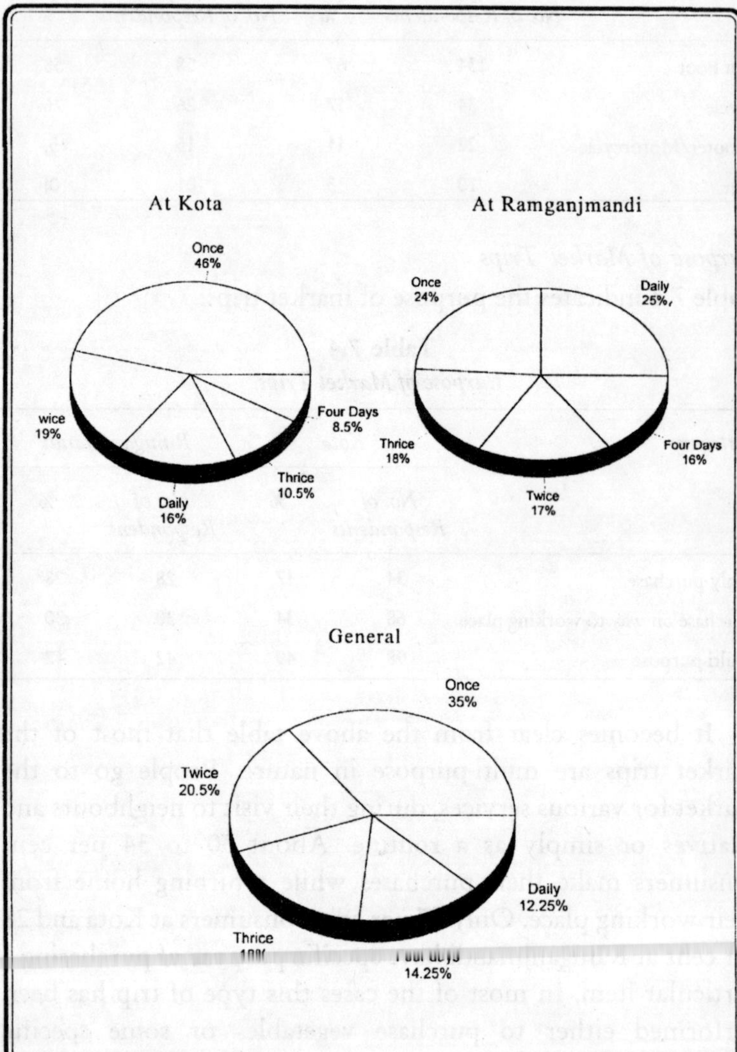

Choice of Shopping Centre

The controlling factor of retail marketing in urban centres is the choice of a particular shop or a shopping centre. In this respect consumer behaviour varies from person to person depending upon his status in terms of income, level of literacy, preferences, social contact, etc. The other factors affecting choice are layout of the shopping centre, size of shop, accessibility to main road, space within centre, location relative to other competing centres, customer base, credit facility, parking facility, etc. It has been observed that most of the consumers shop as a routine but locational aspect, behaviour of shopkeepers and credit facility have a direct impact on choice of a particular shop.

In fact, in the region under study consumerism has not yet developed, therefore, consumers never think in terms of behavioural and infrastructural aspects. But soon, the time will come when retail marketing will be controlled by consumer behaviour.

Behavioural Pattern of Market-Place Participants in Periodic (Weekly) Markets

As described earlier, weekly markets known as *hats* are the rural trading institutions in the Central Hadaoti region. In these markets, market participants are the key components, which make these market-places effective functional units as well as places of social and economic interaction. The behavioural pattern of market participants is the most important factor in the existence and functioning of weekly markets not only in the region under study but in whole of the country. Among market participants in weekly markets traders, middleman and consumers are most important, while many people attend the weekly market just as routine or just as 'bystanders and passersby'. In most of the cases traders also act as middlemen. Therefore, the behavioural pattern of traders and consumers have been examined. The present analysis is based on field work conducted in eight weekly markets, viz., Kota, Ramganjmandi, Dara, Suket, Sangod, Sumerganjmandi, Pipalda and Digod.

Figure 7.3

Urban Consumer's Mode of Travel Used for Shopping

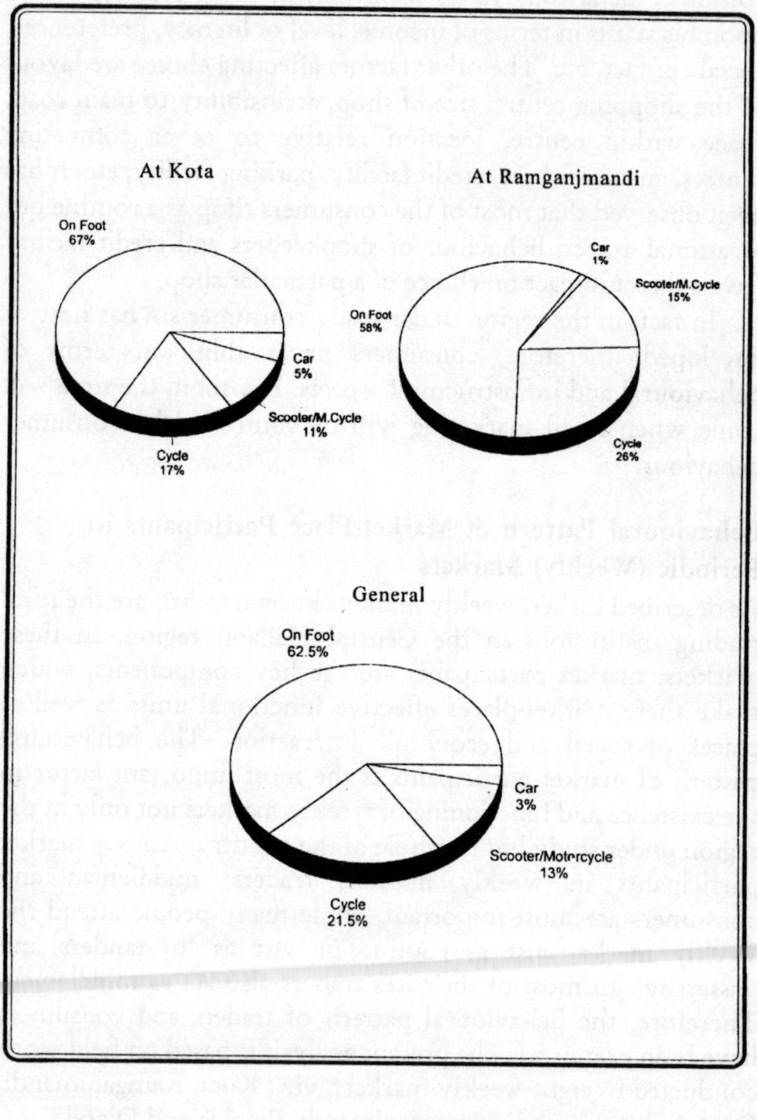

Figure 7.4

Urban Consumer's Purpose of Market Trips

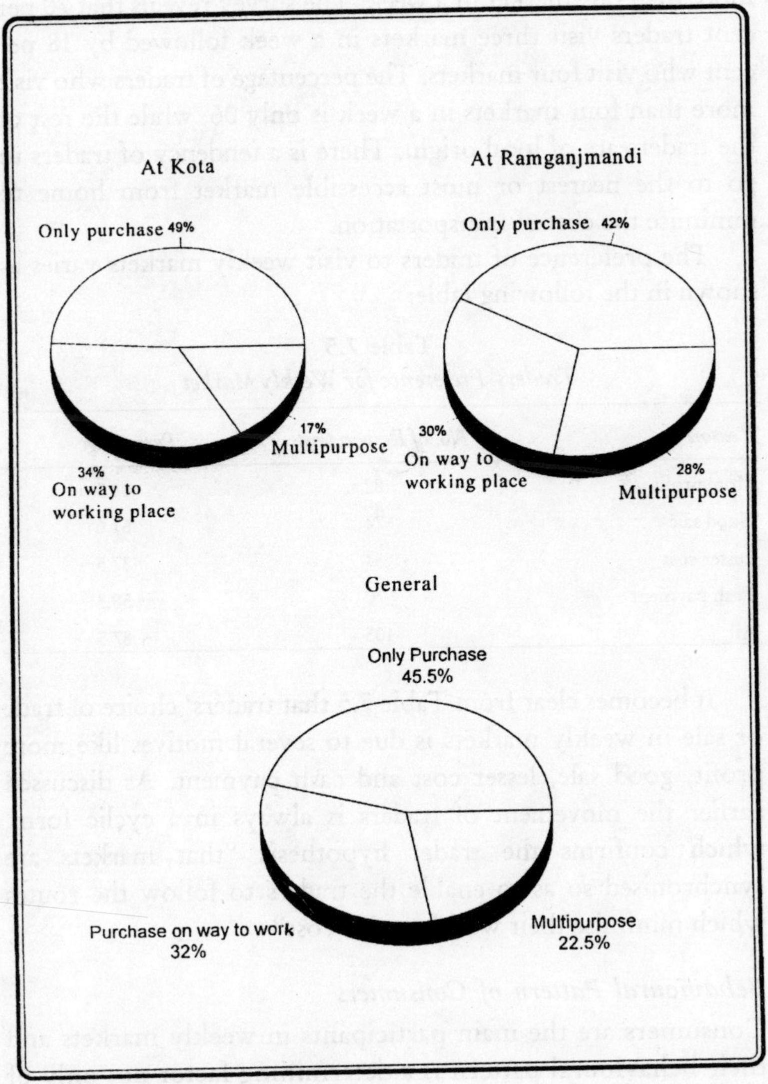

Behavioural Pattern of Traders

In weekly markets traders act as mobile traders. In these markets more than 70 per cent traders are mobile and they visit more than one market in a week. The survey reveals that 70 per cent traders visit three markets in a week followed by 18 per cent who visit four markets. The percentage of traders who visit more than four markets in a week is only 06, while the rest of the traders are of local origin. There is a tendency of traders to go to the nearest or most accessible market from home to minimise the cost of transportation.

The preference of traders to visit weekly markets varies as shown in the following table:

Table 7.5
Traders' Preference for Weekly Market

Reason	*No. of Respondents*	*Percentage*
More profit	82	68.3
Good sale	74	61.6
Lesser cost	54	37.5
Cash payment	70	58.3
All	105	87.5

It becomes clear from Table 7.5 that traders' choice of trade or sale in weekly markets is due to several motives like more profit, good sale, lesser cost and cash payment. As discussed earlier the movement of traders is always in a cyclic form, which confirms the trader hypothesis "that markets are synchronised so as to enable the traders to follow the routes which minimise their weekly travel cost".

Behavioural Pattern of Consumers

Consumers are the main participants in weekly markets and their behavioural pattern is a determining factor not only of the present status of market but for their future existence. In weekly markets most of the rural consumers are also sellers. The following table (Table 7.6) shows the purpose of their visit to markets.

Table 7.6
Purpose of Visit to Weekly Markets

Purpose	*No. of Respondents*	*Percentage*
To sell	115	76.6
To buy	132	88.0
Both	105	70.0
Neither for sale nor purchase	12	08.0

It becomes clear from the above table that 70 per cent consumers attend these markets both for sale and purchase, while 88 per cent go there to buy and 76.6 per cent to sell. In fact, most of the villagers bring small quantities of farm products, which they sell and then they purchase the required goods.

Why do consumers visit the weekly market? The preference for weekly market has been indicated in the following table (Table 7.7):

Table 7.7
Preference for Purchase in Weekly Markets

Reason	*No. of Respondents*	*Percentage*
Cheaper goods	82	68.3
Availability of all goods	74	61.6
Fresh farm products	54	37.5
Personal contact with traders	70	58.3
As part of habit	105	87.5

It becomes clear that most of the rural consumers make their purchases in weekly markets as a habit, mainly because of the availability of all types of goods at one place at low prices. The personal contact with traders has also been a reason which increases with regular visits. With this contact they can avail of credit facility.

Apart from marketing, weekly markets are also a place of social contact. The rural folk also attend these markets for social contact, settlement of marriages, settlement of disputes, for entertainment, etc. Nowadays, political leaders also use these markets for their meetings specially during election period.

The periodicity of the weekly markets is also fixed in consideration with consumers. As Hill and Smith (1972: 348) observed, "markets are synchronised so as to enable the consumers to have easiest possible access to market throughout the week". In general, the behavioural pattern of participants in weekly markets is determined by factors like nearness to market, easy accessibility, profitability and socio-economic relations.

Behavioural Pattern of Participants in Agricultural Markets

Agricultural marketing as a business activity involves the flow of goods and services from the point of initial production to the ultimate consumer. In other words, it is a functional process observed in trading agricultural commodities mainly between producers and traders and indirectly consumers also. As described earlier, in the region under study regulated agricultural marketing is in practice in which the important participants are producer-sellers (farmers) and commission agents/traders. The other participants are brokers, weightmen, hammals, marketing committee officials and government agencies, but their role is fixed. In present section, the behavioural pattern of farmers and traders/commission agents has been examined.

Figure 7.5

(a) Consumer's Purpose of Visit to Weekly Markets
(b) Consumer's Preference for Purchase in Weekly Markets

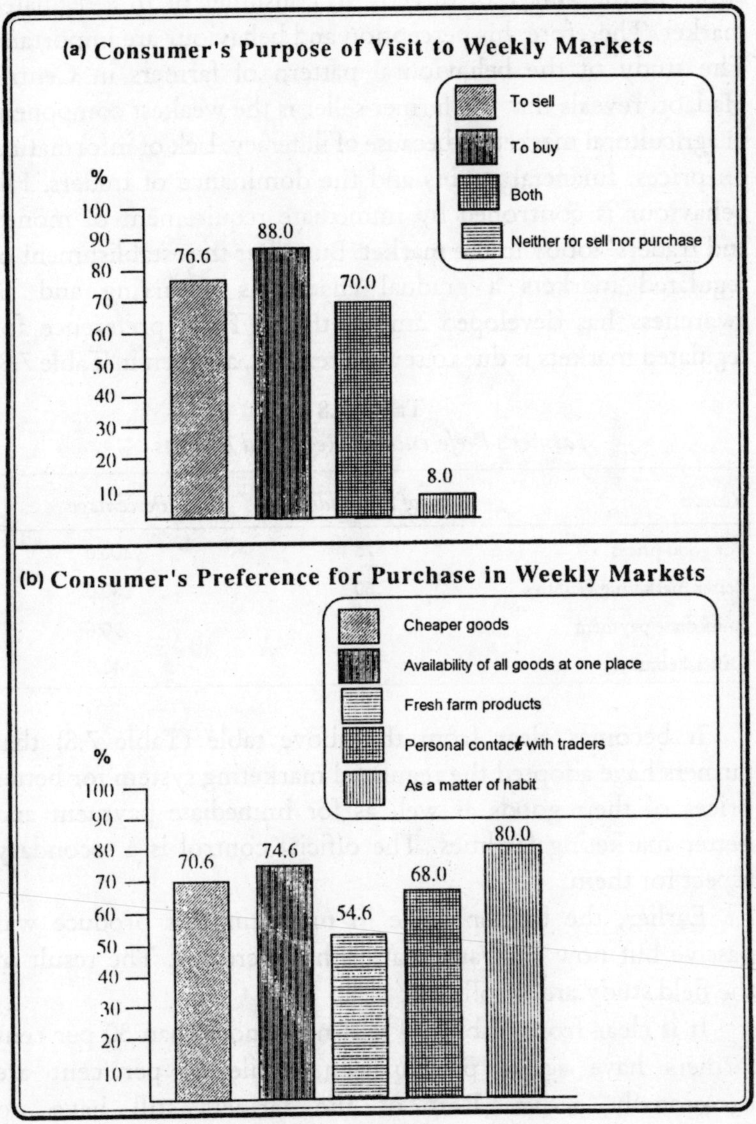

Seller's (Farmer) Behavioural Pattern

The farmer or the producer-seller plays a key role in agricultural marketing. It is the farmer who sells the surplus production either in the village or directly to consumer or in a regulated market. Therefore, his perception and behaviour are important. The study of the behavioural pattern of farmers in Central Hadaoti reveals that the farmer-seller is the weakest component in agricultural marketing because of illiteracy, lack of information on prices, financial strains and the dominance of traders. His behaviour is controlled by immediate requirement of money and traders' lobby in the market. But, after the establishment of regulated markets a gradual change is occurring and an awareness has developed among them. Their preference for regulated markets is due to several reasons, as given in Table 7.8.

Table 7.8

Farmer's Preference for Regulated Markets

Reason	*No. of Respondents*	*Percentage*
For good prices	75	100.0
Better marketing facilities	60	80.0
Immediate payment	68	90.6
Official control	30	40.0

It becomes clear from the above table (Table 7.8) that farmers have adopted the regulated marketing system for better prices of their goods as well as for immediate payment and better marketing facilities. The official control is a secondary aspect for them.

Earlier, the farmer's role in marketing his produce was passive but now his participation has increased. The result of the field study are as follows:

It is clear from Table 7.9 that now more than 50 per cent farmers have active participation, while 24 per cent are occasionally active. Rest of the farmers still have no participation mainly because of illiteracy as well as his indebtedness to a particular trader.

Table 7.9
Farmer's Participation in Marketing

Category	*No. of Respondents*	*Percentage*
Active	41	54.66
Occasionally active	18	24.00
No participation	16	21.34

In brief, farmers' behavioural pattern supports the hypothesis that regulated marketing is beneficial to them. With the increase in awareness it will become more beneficial to them; only then will the objective of the establishment of regulated markets be fullfilled.

Trader's/Commission Agent's Behavioural Pattern

In a regulated marketing system commission agents known as *Arthia* and traders play a vital role and controls the whole system. In most of the cases commission agent also act as traders. Prior to regulated marketing the agents and traders had full monopoly over the system and they used to conduct the marketing of agricultural marketing in the way that suited them they like best. But now they have to follow the rules and regulation of the *mandi* committee. At Kota *mandi* a survey of 50 trader-cum-agents indicates that about 50 per cent traders prefer regulated marketing, while 22 per cent are in favour of the traditional system; for rest it makes no difference.

Similarly there is a general feeling among traders that regulated marketing is an extra channel in marketing and has been developed for the benefit of farmers. But at the same time all of them are of the opinion that now agricultural marketing has become systematic and market yards have given them several facilities which were not available to them earlier. In general, commission agents as well as traders of the region have developed interest in regulated marketing, in spite of certain checks imposed on them by administration.

Synthesis: The behavioural pattern of market-place participants in the region under study is responsible for spatial linkages within and between markets. In periodic markets such linkages have been established in the form of 'market cycles' and movement of consumers in nearby markets, while in regulated markets spatial interaction is established between markets and villages located in the market area. Urban markets are the best examples of spatial relationship between town and its countryside and the consumers provide a strong link in this relationship.

The behavioural pattern of consumers in urban markets is very complex because of the considerable difference in behaviour due to socio-economic factors like varied nature of demand, level of literacy, income, status, mode of transport, specialisation of market, behaviour of shopkeepers, etc. In a periodic market, there is little variation in behaviour of traders and consumer. The very existence of periodic markets depends upon the behavioural pattern of their participants. In agricultural marketing also the behavioural pattern of traders, agents and producer sellers has changed with the market regulation. The present analysis provides a base for the planning of urban, rural and agricultural marketing on the basis of behavioural patterns.

References

Davies, R.L. (1976), *Marketing Geography*, Methuen.

Downs, R.M. (1970), The Cognitive Structure of an Urban Shopping Centre, *Environment and Behaviour*, 2, 1, pp. 13-38.

Hill, P. and Smith, R.H.T. (1972), The Spatial and Temporal Synchronization of Periodic Markets: Evidence from Four Emirates in Northern Nigeria, *Economic Geography*, Vol. 48 (3), pp. 345-55.

Chapter 8

Impact of Marketing Activity on Environment

Marketing activities are the integral part of economic development and like any other developmental activity, they have an impact on regional and/or local ecology, thereby also responsible for several environmental problems. Growth is essentially an economic concept. Production and consumption constitute the elemental units of growth and the growth process is set to move through commercialisation, while consumption is the ultimate objective of all economic activity. Commercialisation facilitates producers to produce more and to reach consumers through the mechanism of marketing-a mechanism involving the whole complex of processes that intervene between production and consumption. All these activities represent an organisational and institutional business. Every organisational and institutional business needs some *situs* or space. This *situs* develops in the form of a commercial complex. A commercial complex may signify a point of location of organised infrastructures of human activities generating and sustaining the necessary mechanism of exchange involving bargain, negotiation equation between either directly producer and consumer or through trader. The place where commercial complexes have developed and where marketing is performed is a market-place, which may be periodic, daily, local, regional, wholesale, and retail. Whatever may be its form market centres are always an integral part of the ecosystem. The ecological complex is a key to the unfolding not only growth of the markets (as described in chapter III) but also its present state and future development.

It is not only the growth of market-places and marketing which have had its background in regional ecological framework but these activities (marketing and its associated activities) also have their effect on the environment, which is a cause of concern for marketing geographers. The impact of marketing activity on the environment has now drawn attention but till now geographers have not done any study directly related with this aspect. This is because of the fact that data regarding this aspect are not available and also because this problem is more in urban areas, where marketing activities are more complex, while vast areas of the countryside still maintains a balance between commercial activities and the environment. However, it is high time not only to take a note of the various facets of marketing activity but also to examine its impact on the environment. The present chapter has been designed to discuss the impact of marketing activity on the environment, both in urban and rural areas.

Impact of Marketing Activity on Urban Environment

Marketing activity and market institutions are ubiquitous to urban development. "Economically defined, the city is a settlement, the inhabitants of which live primarily off trade and commerce rather than agriculture" (Weber, 1958: 65-66). It is difficult to establish whether marketing activity determines the man-made geographic structure of the towns or the structure of the town determines the marketing activity. The urban landscape is always dominated by commercial establishments and there are no two opinions of the fact that larger the town more will be the commercial activities. These commercial activities have had their impact on the environment and create certain problems.

The impact of commercial activity on the environment is more in larger towns. In the Central Hadaoti region, the following towns have been identified in 1991 census:

Table 8.1

Towns of Central Hadaoti (1991)

Towns	*Population*
1. Kota	5,37,371
2. Ramganjmandi	20,875
3. Kaithoon	16,040
4. Sangod	15,603
5. Suket	11,056
6. Satalkheri	9,742
7. Udaipura	6,073

It becomes clear from Table 8.1 that Kota is the largest urban centre of the region which ranks third in towns of the Rajasthan State. Since other towns are very small the impact of marketing activity on environment has been examined in detail for Kota. In other towns also marketing activity has influenced the local landscape, but only to a very limited extent.

The commercial land use in towns is a complex areal phenomenon. This is the space mainly used for commercial purposes, i.e., retail and wholesale markets, storage, banks and insurance. "The spatial pattern of commercial activity inside the city continues to be dominated by a concentration of largest and most important business establishments in the main centre, or central area or central business district (CBD). Throughout the rest of the urban area there seems to be a rather haphazard arrangement of mainly retail activities grouped together in different kinds of business configurations" (Davies, 1976: 117). The three urban land use models developed by a sociologist, a

land economist and two geographers indicates the importance of commercial land use in the city. These three models are:
(i) Concentric Zone Model by Ernest W. Burgess,
(ii) Sector Model by Homer Hoyt, and
(iii) Multiple-Nuclei Model by Harris and Ullman.

In all the models the CBD occupies the prime location. Another approach of the study of urban land use is the ecological one, in which variables of ecological complex have been discussed as outlined by Schnore (1965) and earlier by Duncan (1964) under the following points:

Schnore		*Duncan*
Environment	Topography	Site
Technology	Transport and communication	Accessibility
	The friction of space	
Population	Size	
	Rate of growth	Growth
	Ethnic and racial composition	
Organisation	Economic base	
	Community (ecological) Organisation	Persistence
	Social class composition	

(Quoted by Carter, H., *The Study of Urban Geography*, Edward Arnold, 1976, p. 192).

The whole system of marketing and its infrastructure is always determined by the ecological complex. With the development of market morphology and marketing activity, their impact on environment can be seen. In the region under study market morphology of towns have five components, viz., (i) central business area (ii) secondary business area, (iii) principal business arteries, (iv) connecting business arteries, and (v) isolated clusters. These components are apparent at Kota and Ramganjmandi but in other towns only the main market and their connecting streets can be seen. Whatever may be the form their impact on urban environment is always there.

The growth of commercial areas and growth of population are closely related. In fact, the growth of population creates more demand for goods and services, and is thus responsible for the development of commercial areas/market-places and the net result of this process can be seen on the impact on urban ecosystem. The largest urban centre of the region is Kota and its population has been increasing at a fast rate as indicated in the following table:

Table 8.2
Population of Kota, 1901-91

Census Year	*Population*	*Percentage change*
1901	33,700	
1911	30,300	- 4.2
1921	31,700	+ 1.9
1931	37,400	+ 18.0
1941	47,300	+ 26.5
1951	65,100	+ 37.6
1961	120,345	+ 84.9
1971	213,006	+ 77.0
1981	346,923	+ 62.9
1991	537,371	+ 59.0

According to an estimate, in 1991 the total commercial areas of Kota was 3.4 per cent of the city area in the following form:

Table 8.3
Commercial Areas of Kota, 1991

1. Central business area	50 acres approx.
2. Sub-city centre (excluding wholesale & warehousing)	130 acres approx.
3. District centres	75 acres approx.
4. Sub-district centre and other commercial areas	55 acres approx.
5. Wholesale markets, warehousing and storage depots	210 acres approx.
Total	520 acres approx.

Source: Master Plan Kota, 1971-92. pp. 30.

It becomes clear from Tables 3.2 and 8.3, that population growth has given rise to marketing activities and in turn, is responsible for the degradation of environment. The present analysis of the impact of commercial/marketing activity on urban environment is based on field work conducted at Kota.

When growth of commercial establishments is not according to the demand of growing population, it always creates problems in urban areas including environmental problems. This problem is apparent at Kota, because when market-places developed mostly in pre-independence period the population was limited and most of the markets have been developed within the walled city along the main road from Ladpura to Patanpol. But when pressure increased the side lanes have been used as markets. But after the fifties, the growing pressure of population was so much that these markets have become very congested. This is not only the problem of Kota but common to all the urban centres. This problem is more because of unplanned growth and unauthorised occupation of land by shopkeepers, who use an unauthorised platform in front of their shop to display their goods. As a result, unhealthy conditions develop due to traffic and crowd. At Kota, in markets like Bajaj Khana, Behru Gali, Old Grain Market, Sunder Dharamshala market, Ghantaghar market, Patanpol and other markets located in old city the environmental conditions are not hygienic to residents as well as to shopkeepers and other workers. Outside the city, conditions are better but they are degrading day by day with the growing pressure of population.

In cities, marketing and its associated activities are also responsible for the degradation of the urban environment in the form of air and noise pollution, and dumping of waste material.

With the growing marketing activities the problem of air pollution is increasing day by day. Since markets are congested and without proper parking space, the problem of air pollution grows. This problem is more evident in the walled city.

Noise pollution is mainly due to horn of the vehicles as well as due to the loud voices of the vendors. Since most of the markets are congested the use of the horn (some time pressure horn) creates unbearable noise. Advertisement of products with loudspeakers is also a main cause of noise pollution not only in Kota but in other small market towns of the region.

The problem of waste disposal is today a growing problem in market-places and is directly responsible for land pollution. Generally shopkeepers throw waste material in front of their own shops or at some nearby open space. This waste contains paper, cardboard, poly packs, cloth pieces, etc. In shops preparing and selling juices and edibles, a huge quantity of waste is thrown daily. So also in vegetable, fruit and meat markets. Since there is no provision for waste disposal, it creates land and air pollution and becomes the cause of diseases. Because of waste products clogging the drains, the local drainage system in markets fail aggravating the pollution problem.

The marketing activities are also responsible for unhealthy conditions within shops. In urban markets because of high land value shops are small without proper ventilation facilities. This affects the health of shopkeepers as well as of the consumers. The conditions in godowns are worse and unhealthy. These are dark and damp rooms without any ventilation. Tuberculosis and asthma are common ailments among the labourers working there.

There is a tendency to convert the front portion of the residential house into shops. This happens not only in main markets but in residential colonies also. The purpose of this is to get extra income. But this affects the lives of the families and also creates environmental problems for the entire colony. At Kota several colonies such as Vigyan Nagar, Talwandi, Mahaveer Nagar, Gumanpura, Bhimmandi, etc., face problems of traffic congestion and pollution due to conversion of front portion of the house into shops.

A periodic market (weekly market) is a gathering of buyers and sellers at an appointed place and time, usually between 10 a.m. and 6 p.m. These markets attract a large number of buyers and sellers and when there is a gathering of 500 to 3,000 people, some environmental problems crop up.

The weekly markets are held: (i) along the main road of the settlement, (ii) along approach road, (iii) at a central place of the settlement, and (iv) at an open space. Whatever may be the location, the space is very limited. On market day the whole area becomes a congested place full of temporary shops, spread on both sides of the road or in a rectangular manner. This already congested space becomes unmanageably suffocating and unpleasant when a large crowd of buyers comes in. The result of this can be seen in the form of air and noise pollution for about five to six hours of market time. The whole market area and its adjoining regions is enveloped in a blanket of dust, creating the problem of air pollution.

Noise pollution is caused by the vendors shouting for their products and loudspeakers blaring in full volume. Waste disposal also is a major cause for concern.

In spite of the above mentioned environmental problems created by weekly markets, these markets are quite sustainable from the ecological point of view because:

(i) the time involved in these markets is very short,

(ii) there are no permanent shops and other establishment,

(iii) the pattern of 'market shift' provides complete spatial interaction in the region,

(iv) the commodity structure of these markets is according to the needs of the local environment, and

(v) these markets are not only marketing institutions but more of a social institution and an integral part of the cultural ecology.

It has been observed that whatever damage to environment has been done during marketing hours in these markets is recovered during the next six days. Therefore, the weekly markets are ecologically suitable.

Another institution of periodic marketing is the fair known as *mela*. The fairs are ancient trading and social institutions. They are held once or twice a year and are generally associated with festivals or religious places. In Central Hadaoti region, as we have seen earlier, 48 fairs are held, and the gathering in these fairs is larger than in periodic markets. This crowd is responsible for air, water and noise pollution. The dust and smoke of vehicles creates atmospheric pollution. In the region many cattle fairs are also held in which cattle aggravate the level of pollution. Noise pollution is created by loudspeakers, singers, dancers as well as by the common people, while water pollution is a main problem in the vicinity of the fairs. Most of the fairs are held either near a tank, a well or a river. Generally demand of water is more and its availability is limited therefore water becomes polluted. The same water is used for bathing and drinking purposes by cattle also. This polluted water becomes the cause of concern to authorities when diseases like cholera spread. There is no provision for waste disposal. In fairs heaps of waste can be seen here and there. It includes human and animal waste as well as waste cleared from shops.

Since periodicity of fairs is limited, their impact on environment is also short term. What is needed is proper arrangement for drinking water and waste disposal.

In brief, the problem of environmental degradation due to marketing activities is not a serious problem in the region under study. Kota city is an example of the environmental impact of marketing activity on urban environment. In other urban centres this problem is not so serious. Similarly, in rural areas, periodic markets are economically viable, ecologically sound and socially acceptable. For long term planning of market-places, there is a need for sustainable development. The development of more periodic markets in rural areas will be a major step towards sustainable development of markets and marketing.

References

Davies, Ross L. (1976), *Marketing Geography*, Methuen and Co. London.

Duncan, B. (1964), 'Variables in Urban Morphology', in E.W. Burgess and D.J. Bogue, eds. *Contributions to Urban Sociology*, Chicago.

Schnore, L.F. (1965), 'On the Spatial Structure of Cities in the two Americas', in P.M. Hauser and L.F. Schnore, eds., *The Study of Urbanization*, New York, pp. 353-4.

Chapter 9

Problems of Marketing and Planning for Sustainable Development

The study of the various facets of markets and marketing in Central Hadaoti region reveals that there is an urgent need to broadbase our development planning in terms of time and space. For planned economic development several efforts have been made and considerable progress has been recorded in various sectors of economy like agriculture, irrigation, industries, mining, transportation and trade. But least attention has been given to the systematic growth and development of market centres and marketing system. Apart from the growth of regulated agricultural markets no efforts have been made for the development of urban and rural markets, which is very essential for integrated growth of regional economy. Another aspect of the planning of marketing is that it should be ecologically sustainable for which geographical study in terms of spatial analysis provides a base both for short-term and long-term planning.

The development strategy of market centres is one of the several ways to deal with regional planning. Market centres are not only the centres of marketing activity but they are also the

nerve centres of development Market centres are also important because they are:
(i) human settlement, either urban or rural;
(ii) centres of economic and social activity;
(iii) central service centres;
(iv) nodes of transportation; and
(v) the controllers of marketing activity.

The growth of market centres are complementary to other economic activities. Therefore, there is a need for the planning and sustainable development of marketing in the region under study. But before planning, the problems of marketing should be discussed, so that a proper planning strategy can be evolved.

PROBLEMS

The problems associated with marketing in Central Hadaoti region can be divided into the following three broad categories:
(i) problems of urban markets,
(ii) problems of periodic markets, and
(iii) problems of agricultural markets.

Problems of Urban Markets or Market Towns

In the region there are only eight market towns, viz., Kota, Ramganjmandi, Sangod, Kaithoon, Suket, Itawa, Sultanpur and Sumerganjmandi. Among these towns Kota is the largest market town not only of the region but of the state, thus facing several problems, while other market towns are smaller and accordingly their problems of marketing are also limited. The main problems of the market towns are as follows:

1. *Congested market-places*: All the market towns of the region are unplanned and market-places are located along the main road as well as in narrow side lanes. With the growth of population, the number of consumers has increased manifold, but the basic layout of markets and structure of shops has remained unchanged. This problem is more in Kota, where most of the markets are still located within the walled city and

are very congested. Ramganjmandi is also facing the same problem. This congestion is also a cause of pollution especially during peak hours of shopping, i.e., between 4 p.m. to 8 p.m.

2. *Lack of parking space*: Due to congestion and unplanned growth of market-places, there is no provision for parking space. There is a tendency to park vehicles in front of the shop itself. This creates great difficulty to consumers, pedestrians and other vehicle owners also.

3. *Encroachment by shopkeepers*: Shopkeepers display some of their goods on the footpath of the shop. This type of encroachment is increasing day by day particularly at Kota in spite of several steps taken by the local authorities. Because of this consumers face great difficulty in their shopping.

4. *Unhygeinic conditions in and outside the shop*: Except in few shopping centres and showrooms in big cities, the conditions of shops are unhygeinic. There is no provision for fresh air in the shop. Shopkeepers never think about cleanliness of the shop. On the contrary they throw all the waste just in front of their shops. All this create unhygeinic conditions both for shopkeeper as well as to consumers.

5. *Problem of price variations*: The price of similar goods varies from shop to shop creating confusion among the consumers. There is a system to mention price of packed and other goods, but in the absence of uniformity and monitoring system shopkeeper always take advantage and consumers are at loss.

6. *Poor quality and duplicate goods*: Nowadays consumers are facing a great problem of duplicate and poor quality of goods. It is difficult to separate the original from duplicate goods. This is not the problems of illiterate consumers but also of educated consumers. In fact, a parallel trade of duplicate goods is going on for the sake of greater profit at the cost of quality.

7. *Malpractice in weights and measures*: In spite of laws regulating weights and measures, many shopkeepers do not use standard weights and measures. This is common in the big

shops, petrol pumps and others establishments. The consumers are helpless, because in most cases they are oblivious of the reality. These practices are more common in small towns where most of the consumers are of rural origin.

8. *Adulteration of food items*: The problem of adulteration is a major cause for concern specially in food items like oil, ghee, spices, wheat flour, gram flour, pulses, seeds and other items. This affects the consumers' health and often is the cause of disease.

9. *Misleading advertisements*: Advertisements often mislead the consumers. Although advertisements help the consumer to select good quality of goods, in many cases the goods mentioned in advertisement do not have the mentioned standard.

10. *Lack of display facility*: Except in a few big stores at Kota, there is no provision for display of goods outside the shop. In the absence of that consumers generally face difficulties in selection of goods.

11. *Unplanned expansion of markets*: In the region under study market towns are expanding in an unplanned manner in order to fulfil the growing demands of consumers. Local authorities never pay attention to this type of expansion, which in future will definitely create problems for people as well as to city planners.

In brief, market towns of the Central Hadaoti region need immediate attention for a healthy and efficient marketing system. The situation at Kota is the worst, therefore, immediate steps should be taken for the improvement in marketing environment of the city.

Problems of Periodic Markets

Every periodic market is having its own specific problems related either to site, space, structure, trading, administration, etc. Apart from these specific problems, there are general problems also prevalent throughout the region which require immediate attention to ameliorate the marketing facilities. The following problems have been identified as general problems of periodic markets and/or marketing system of the region.

Locational Problems

The site of the periodic market should be an advantageous location which will provide for the growth and development but with the growth of population and expansion of habitation as well as due to urbanisation several periodic markets are now facing the problems of poor location. The main problem related with site is either accessibility or shortage of space. The growing pressure of permanent market is also one of the main reasons which creates site problems. At Kota, the site of the weekly market has been shifted from Sunder Dharamshala area to Bhimmandi area because of excessive congestion on market day. Ramganjmandi, Dara, Sangod, Indergarh and Digod are also facing similar problems but not able to shift due to lack of alternative space.

Problem of Space

All the periodic markets which exist today have grown from the pre-independence period when the population was limited and there was no problem of space. But during the last thirty years most of the periodic markets in the region are facing the problem of space. The congested streets of the village or a town do not provide sufficient opportunities for proper display of goods and their marketing as well as for other special activities associated with periodic marketing. This is not only the problem of periodic markets held in towns but also in rural areas, where space for the market is not available within the habitation and the surrounding area generally is an agricultural area which nobody is ready to give for this purpose.

Infrastructural Problems

It is said that periodic markets are temporary markets without any infrastructure, but this is a wrong notion. In fact, periodic markets also have infrastructure in the form of arrangement of shops, facilities for parking, social gathering, place for sale and purchase of cattle, etc. The arrangement of shops is generally in a fixed pattern and entry of a new shopkeeper is more or less restricted by the regular shopkeepers. In most of the periodic markets there are sections of similar type of shops but due to rapid growth in number of shops this pattern has been disturbed in many markets, because of which, the overall structure has become complex demanding rectification in the form of space for shopkeepers. Similarly, the small producer-sellers are not having fixed sites because of their irregularity. The lack of parking space is a very common problem in all the weekly markets where a large number of bullock carts, other cattle, cycles arrive. Sometimes mobile traders create problem in already congested markets. There are problems of drinking water both for men and cattle, no place for social gathering, lack of emergency first aid facilities and police check post, etc. Since a token fee is collected by local authorities it is their duty to provide at least the minimum infrastructural facilities to market participants.

Problems of Market Participants

The main participants of periodic markets are producer-sellers, mobile traders, middlemen and consumers. Although periodic markets are beneficial to all the market participants there are certain problems which need rectification and improvement for proper functioning of these marketing institutions.

Problems of Producer-Sellers

Periodic markets provide an opportunity to small farmers as well as to tribals to sell small quantities of their produce in these markets. They first sell these products and then purchase the required goods. Since these producer-sellers are unorganised, they do not get price for their goods and become victims of either middlemen or traders. Sometimes their produce is sold to middlemen in less than half its prevalent price. This type of exploitation of farmers and tribals should be checked immediately by government authorities. The producers of earthenwares, bamboo-baskets, and other handicrafts products are also not getting a fair price. In these markets barter system is also prevalent and generally, the producer-seller does not get a commodity in proportion to his commodity. The indebtedness of producer-sellers is also one of the reasons to sell their produce at a cheaper rate. Another reason is the shortage of time at their disposal because they must dispose of their produce and only then purchase the required articles within the short span of three or four hours.

Problems of Traders

In periodic markets the trader may be both local and outside ones. Generally local traders are well placed and face minimum problems but outside traders face several problems like: (1) accessibility to market-place, (2) mode of travel, (3) space for display of their products, and (4) aggressive attitude of the local administration.

Problems of Middlemen

In periodic markets middlemen are always at an advantageous position because they purchase goods from producers at very cheap price and sell to the traders at a large profit margin. But even these middlemen are facing certain difficulties due to increasing awareness among villagers. Another problem is the lack of coordination among themselves. Generally, they sit along the entrance point of weekly markets and since they are rival competitors, they do not have co-ordination and co-operation. There is also the pressure from the local administration as also from traders and producers urging them to reduce their exploitative attitude.

Problems of Consumers

Consumers are the main and largest participants of the periodic market. In fact, periodic markets are primarily meant for the fulfilment of the demands of the consumer scattered in several villages located around these market centres. The problems associated with consumers are: (1) price variations, (2) variations in quality of goods, and (3) high rate of interest charged by traders on the loan given in the form of commodities. The hapless consumers are also victims of the traders but this is not a serious problem and gradually due to literacy and awareness this problem is on the decline and in times to come the consumers will dominate the scene. Other problems of consumers are the lack of shade during rest time, non-availability of drinking water, medical facilities, etc. But it is certain that despite these problems periodic markets are beneficial to consumers.

Problems of Law and Order

Those participants who visit the market just for fun sometimes create problems of law and order, particularly in tribal markets where young boys and girls move here and there in the market in search of a partner. In tribal families disputes are settled in these markets so there is always the fear of disturbing the law and order situation.

Problems of Pollution

In rural areas where there is no *pucca* road for movement of people and vehicles, there is a lot of air pollution. Due to absence of proper drainage, stagnant water can be seen in low lying areas creating an unhealthy atmosphere. In tribal markets the participants are not aware of general hygiene therefore, there are unhealthy conditions prevailing in such markets.

Problems of Regulated Marketing

The regulated marketing system is quite successful in the state as well as in the region under study, providing several facilities to farmers and traders. But there are several problems and lacunae connected with the system. The present study reveals the problems associated with farmers and traders:

1. Problems Faced by the Farmers

Regulated agricultural marketing system has been directed towards the benefit of farmers and many problems faced by them prior to the establishment of regulated markets have been either solved or minimised. However, some of the problems still faced by farmers are as follows:

(1) lack of storage facility and quick post-harvest disposal of produce,
(2) the problem of quick and cheap transportation,
(3) delay in weighment and auction,
(4) the problem of supervision of the produce in the market,
(5) the problem of delayed payment,
(6) the problem of price variation,
(7) financial problems,
(8) unauthorised deductions and multiplicity of charges, and
(9) inadequate market intelligence.

(i) Storage problem

The storage requirement is of two types: (i) temporarily the produce is to be stored by the farmer till it is transported to the market, and (ii) storage for a longer period for uniform distribution of supply according to demand. Facilities in both aspects are inadequate in the region. As a result, farmers are forced to sell their produce as soon as the harvest is over, thus creating a glut in the market due to heavy inflow of produce at this time. During these two months farmers are always the ones to lose because of the downward trend of prices.

(ii) Transportation problem

In spite of considerable development of road transportation, a large number of villages are not connected with metalled roads. The regulated markets committees have constructed link road in their respective market areas, but many villages are still without them. As a result the producer farmers face great difficulties in transporting their produce on bullock-carts to markets which are often situated at long distances.

(iii) Delay in cleaning, weighment and auction

The farmers are usually in a hurry to sell their produce in the market in order to meet their need for cash. Therefore, there is sudden inflow of supplies in the market during the post-harvest period of two to three months. This creates congestion in market yard, leading to delays in cleaning and weighment of the produce.

Apart from this, delay in auction of the produce also causes inconvenience and harassment of the farmers. During the peak season of post-harvest the arrivals are heavy, and within a short period it is not possible that auction of every lot is done.

(iv) The problem of supervision

Until the produce is sold, the seller has to stay at the commission agents' shop to ensure that there are no losses due to pilferage, damage or through wrong weighment. Pilferage in small quantities and occasional theft are not uncommon in the absence of proper check posts. Stray cattle are also found in these markets. Besides, damage is often caused to the produce by occasional rains and storms. Therefore, for proper supervision of their produce, the farmers have to remain in the market till the produce is sold.

(v) Delayed payment

The delay in payment to farmers was more a problem of the pre-regulation period. In spite of the provision of immediate payment in full to farmers, traders often delayed it for one reason or another. This practice is more during the peak period, when immediate full payment was not made for want of sufficient funds by commission agents.

(vi) The problem of price variation

The variation in prices of the same commodity in the markets located within a region or a district, is a cause of dissatisfaction among farmers. Low prices was a common feature in the small town markets. This is mainly because the number of traders are limited and they monopolise the marketing scenario. Generally farmers are not aware of the prevalent prices, therefore, they were the losers.

(vii) Lack of grading facilities

On paper, there has been much talk about the grading of agricultural commodities according to their quality. But proper grading facilities are not available. No effort has been made to train farmers for grading their produce. Thus, most farmers bring their produce to the market without grading. Many traders accept that when they sell their produce after grading they get a higher income from it.

(viii) Financial problems

The main reason of farmers' weakness is that most of them are poor. This poverty has forced him to take loans from the *Artiya* (commission agent) or traders and this again indirectly forces him to hand over his product to this agent. The present-day agriculture has become quite expensive because of greater use of agricultural inputs like improved seed, chemical fertilisers, pesticides, etc. Finance is also required for tractors, tubewells, electricity, etc. In most of the cases the farmer is financed by the village trader or by the *mandi artiya* on his own terms and conditions charging high interest rates. Although credit facility has been extended by rural banks and other agencies these are very limited and not available to poor needy farmers.

(ix) Unauthorised deductions and multiplicity of charges

As per the State Marketing Act all unauthorised deductions have been banned. The charges for each marketing activity have also been fixed. But in practice the traders/agents often deduct a fixed percentage on account of impurities ranging from 1 to 5 per cent. Similarly there is this exploitative practice among agents to take a sample of produce from the farmers' lot—the quantity of such sample varies from 200 grams to one kilogram, and when such sample is taken by several traders it results in a net loss to the farmer.

Similarly there is multiplicity of charges. In the market the cultivator has to pay many charges like commission, brokerage, weighment, *hamali*, *karda* (impurity charge) and *dhalta* (excessive moisture charge). Some of these charges have no connection to the farmers. Even in regulated markets farmers charge against the rules, for example traders deduct an unauthorised amount for the weighment, filling charges and also *hamali* (loading charges) from farmers' account. As a result the marketing cost of produce goes up.

(x) Inadequate market intelligence

The producer in the village has little contact with market information. He depends mostly on local rates reported by neighbours and local traders. The village merchants never reveal the correct price prevailing in primary and secondary markets because of their personal interest in buying the produce from farmers at lower price. State-wide arrangements have been made for the publicity of prices of agricultural commodities in the regulated markets, but most of this information is beneficial only to traders. The illiterate farmers are not taken into consideration and most of the information is confusing to him. It is only after reaching the market that the helpless farmer learns from his agent that the quality and type of his produce is not of the particular price level. The traders guild (unofficial) also declares a superfluous higher price in order to attract sellers and when actual auction is done the price comes downs. This is when the producer-seller has no option other than to sell his goods.

(xi) Other problems

Apart from the above mentioned problems, the farmers face difficulties concerned with absence of night halt or stay facility. Lack of cattle sheds, drinking water, sanitation, etc., are also common.

2. Problems Faced by Commission Agents and Traders

A general concept regarding agricultural marketing is that traders and middlemen have the advantage in regulated markets. But our survey reveals that both commission agents and traders also have their problems. These are:

(i) Slow performance of market operations

It has been pointed out by traders of 60 per cent *mandis* that the slow performance of market operations such as clearing, weighment, loading-unloading and lifting is responsible for the congestion in the market. These operations are performed by manual labour and operations of clearing and sieving of produce take up a good deal of time. Similarly, auction of produce also takes up a lot of time.

(ii) Inadequate transportation

Like farmers, traders also face the problem of transportation at three levels: (i) at the local level within the town, (ii) at inter-market level, and (iii) at the inter-state level.

At local market level, the after-sale produce is lifted for loading in the godowns or for delivery to the mill or the railway station. The local transport in the towns is primarily bullock-carts, camel and donkey carts. The transport cost varied from 50 paisa to 75 paisa per quintal according to distance. Due to limited carrying capacity carts used to take long time. Only one per cent traders are using tractor or trucks for local transportation.

At the inter-market level the motor truck transport is extensively in use. It is most convenient but during peak season their limited availability is harmful to traders. For inter-state transport both trucks and rail transport are used. In case of railway availability of wagons is limited and often it takes more time, therefore, now a days traders prefer to send their goods by trucks, but truck unions at many times are not co-operative.

(iii) Costly and inefficient labour

Production technology has contributed to increased demand for agricultural labour. In the past few years wages of unskilled labour have increased, especially in the peak season. All operations, therefore, which require human labour have become costly.

Each regulated market has its own problems, some of which are: (i) problem of accessibility; (ii) lack of proper facilities in market yards; (iii) inadequacy of auction platform; and (iv) problem of cleanliness, drainage repair, street lights, etc.

PLANNING FOR SUSTAINABLE DEVELOPMENT

The question of ecologically sustainable development has gained importance. The rapid growth of urbanisation and commercialisation have had their impact on regional as well as local environment. These problems are more in urban areas, where marketing activities are complex. Vast areas of the countryside are still maintaining a balance between marketing activities and the environment. But it is high time not only to take a note of commercial activities and ecologically sustainable development but also to plan for such development which is economically viable, ecologically sound and socially acceptable.

The planning for sustainable development of market-places and marketing can be done: (i) by suggesting measures to solve the problems of marketing, and (ii) to suggested a strategy of sustainable development.

SUGGESTIONS

For the development of marketing in the Central Hadaoti region, there is an urgent need to solve the prevalent problems. The following steps should be taken to solve or at least minimise the problems of market-places and marketing:

(i) Planning for the Urban Markets

Due to the complex nature of marketing at urban places, several problems have emerged as described earlier. In Central Hadaoti region, Kota is facing several problems related to market infrastructure. Other urban centres are also growing day by day, therefore, steps should be taken to solve these problems. A few suggestions in this direction are as follows:

1. Development of new market-places in order to avoid congestion in existing markets.
2. Check should be imposed on encroachment by shopkeepers. This should be restricted and heavy punishment including imprisonment be imposed on those who flout the rules.
3. Specialised markets in each market be developed. Their size may vary according to the threshold population.
4. In each market parking space be created. If it is not possible within the market, a nearby place be selected for this purpose and strict checks should be observed through traffic police.
5. Awareness programmes should be conducted for all shopkeepers to maintain hygienic environment within and outside their shops. For new shops, opening licence be issued only after inspection for a healthy environment.
6. Price of durable and consumable goods should be displayed on a board as well on the packet of goods. It should be the net price, including all taxes.
7. There must be a check on duplicate goods. It is the duty of the market inspector to check this practice.
8. Strict measures should be taken to restrict food adulteration and heavy penalties imposed, including closure of the shop and imprisonment of owner.
9. Advertisement should depict the reality of the goods rather than make false claims.
10. In new shops, facility of the display of goods should be made compulsory.
11. In each newly built locality provision for shopping centre be made.
12. At Kota a supermarket should be started. The best site for the super market is either in Gumanpura area or at Chawani Choraha.

(ii) Planning for Weekly Markets

In the region under study weekly market centres are the basic building blocks of the complex market-place exchange system of the modern economy. Weekly markets play a vital role in rural economy and provide an opportunity not only for marketing but for social interaction to the rural people. But in the development plans least attention has been given for the planning of weekly markets, mostly because of the lack of awareness about these markets among the policy-makers. In the region these rural markets are functioning very well. A few suggestions for their planning are as follows:

(i) In many villages the space of market ground is insufficient to accommodate the huge gathering of the people. This is due to increase in the size of the village as well as due to a general increase in threshold population. Therefore, the site of the weekly market be shifted a nearby open space, as has been done in the case of urban weekly market at Kota. This is upto the local organisers to judge the suitability of the present site.

(ii) The exploitation of small producers, who bring their products to sell in weekly markets should be checked. Generally, traders and commission agents purchase it at a very low price. This practice must be checked by adopting the following measures:
   (a) proper supervision of local bodies,
   (b) create awareness of the current price structure, when they enter the market, and/or
   (c) purchase of farm products (only non-perishable) by village co-operative societies.

(iii) In spite of standardisation of the weights and measures, many shopkeepers still use traditional balance and weights and take advantage of the illiteracy of rural people. Occasional check of weights and measures will solve this problem.

(iv) The weekly markets can be used as places of extension services for the rural people. New developments in the field of agriculture, medical and health care, etc., can be popularised among the rural folk through these markets.

(v) Local bodies must provide facilities like drinking water, parking space for cattle and vehicles, etc., and also take measures for long-term improvement, such as plantation of trees.

All these steps can be taken for improvement by the local people without any expenditure. Only thing required is the proper orientation towards periodic markets. If local people realise the need for the establishment of a new periodic market that should be done, otherwise there is no need for any super imposition.

(iii) Planning for the Fairs

Fairs are basically rural trading and social institutions. They are also periodic in nature being held once or twice in a year. In spite of their being purely traditional institutions, fairs are not disappearing, rather their importance is increasing. In Central Hadaoti regions the Kota Dashera Fair is an example of the fair as trading institution and its pattern is changing with time. The other fairs are also important in their respective areas. The following suggestions can help in their improvement and further planning:

(i) A complete calendar of fairs held in the region should be prepared, in which information about their schedule, location, motive, nature of trade, etc., be given. This information will be helpful to all participants both regional and inter-regional as well as to the government.

(ii) Since fairs attract a large gathering, proper arrangements should be done for stay, drinking water, transportation, medical care, etc.

(iii) In the region cattle fairs are important not only for regional people but also for other parts of the state as well as of adjoining states. These fairs should be organised in a systematic manner, so that trade in cattle be encouraged.

(iv) Some of the fairs can be developed as tourist fairs. The Dashera fair of Kota is one such, which is peculiar and represents the cultural heritage of the region. The Donkey Fair at Umendganj is a unique fair of the State in which only sale and purchase of donkeys is done. Others fairs can also be of interest at least for the Indian tourist.

(v) Fairs can be used to educate rural people through exhibitions, documentary films, posters and other means of publicity. In big fairs such practice is common today. But this should be done in all fairs. Special emphasis must be given to popular innovations in the field of agriculture. Similarly, knowledge about family planning, health care, environment conservation and other developmental activities can be given.

(iv) Suggestions for Planning of Regulated Marketing

For streamling the agricultural marketing in the region all efforts, both government and allied marketing agencies, should be directed to solving the prevalent problems, and a planned strategy be prepared for future development of regulated agricultural marketing. The following suggestions may be taken into consideration:

(i) *Storage facility for farmers*: Adequate storage facilities are essential to save farmers from exploitation at the time of harvesting. With public agencies entering the market to purchase large quantities of foodgrains and other products, the establishment of adequate warehouses in producing areas has become important. This will enable farmers to store the produce safely in the first instance, avoiding damage due to rains, floods, pilferage and spoilage.

(ii) *Transportation facilities*: A complete development plan should be prepared for rural link road development for the entire region. Similarly, proper inter-market and inter-state transportation be provided in time for the benefit of traders. A scheme for providing free transport facility to small and marginal farmers for transportation of their agricultural produce during harvest season has already been launched recently. Under this scheme KUMS have 'collection centres' in their territorial area, transport the produce to the market yard for sale through open auction. The scheme is very good, if properly implemented.

(iii) *Seasonal glut and price control*: As a result of seasonal glut, farmers sometimes get such a low price as is not even sufficient to recover the cost of inputs. This should be checked at government level under the supervision of *mandi* officials.

(iv) *Farmer's marketing co-operatives be started*: In order to provide strength to unorganised farmers, the farmer's co-operative must be opened. The advantages of farmers co-operative are (i) reduction in the cost of commodity handling, (ii) storage facilities to farmers, (iii) small loans and advances available to farmers, (iv) the producer can be educated about market prices and consumer preferences, (v) the farmer may also succeed in securing trade advantages such as lower transport rates, grading of the produce, and (vi) above all it will be their own organisation. The farmers' co-operative will be more useful to small and marginal farmers.

(v) *Development plans for individual market*: Each regulated market is unique in itself catering to its own problems, which will need proper attention at its own level. Therefore, a directive should be issued to each 'Krishi Upaj Mandi Samiti' to prepare a development plan keeping in view the present and prospective problems and the availability of resources. This will not only help in its planned development but also in proper utilisation of resources.

(vi) *Proper vigilance*: In every regulated market vigilance staff is very limited and usually inefficient, with the result that some malpractices are often adopted by traders. This problem is more in Super 'A' and 'A' class *mandis*. Without disturbing the present system, proper vigilance can be developed through short circuit TV cameras. This system could be installed in the Super 'A' class market of Kota to begin with.

(vii) *Mechanisation*: In agricultural marketing mechanisation be introduced in three stages, i.e., movement of goods from the production point to the market, buying and selling operations, and movement of the produce from market to consumers.

The use of mechanical driers and cleaners should be popularised among producers for quick drying and cleaning of the produce in the yard itself. For weighing, loading and unloading mechanisation devices should be installed at market yards. The *mandi* committee may impose a small levy for such devices as weigh-bridge, bucket elevators, belt conveyors, mechanical graders, etc.

(viii) *Incentives*: In order to attract more sellers and buyers in regulated markets some incentives be given to them. A few suggested incentives are as follows:

- (i) Lower market charges may be levied on small and marginal farmers whose produce constitutes a major portion of the total produce.
- (ii) The KUMS should provide agricultural inputs such as high yielding variety (HYV) seeds, pesticides, fertilisers, etc., at subsidised rates to those farmers who market their produce through regulated market.
- (iii) Transportation, storage facilities to farmers be provided and loan against crops be given to them, if required.

SUSTAINABLE DEVELOPMENT

Every economic activity has had its impact on the environment, and marketing is no exception to it. The impact of marketing activities on the environment has been discussed in Chapter 8. The analysis reveals that all forms of marketing activity, viz., urban, rural (periodic markets, fairs) and agricultural have some adverse effect on the local and regional ecosystem. Therefore, a development strategy should be prepared in such a way that can minimise the impact on the environment. In other words, planning for the 'sustainable development' or 'eco-development' be done, in which all developmental activities are performed or designed in such a way that the regional ecological balance is maintained.

While formulating the market development plan due consideration should be given both to urban and rural marketing, which are complementary to each other. The impact of marketing activity on the environment in urban areas is more as in case of Kota city, in the region under study. For every individual market centre a development plan with environmental consideration should be prepared. This is not only necessary for Kota city but also for other market towns, which are growing at a fast rate. For the region as a whole, the development strategy for marketing should be ecologically sustainable.

In Central Hadaoti region periodic weekly markets are successfully performing marketing functions, because this system has developed in close relationship with ecological complex and is suitable for the rural population. The weekly markets (*hats*) are not only found in rural areas of the region but are also held in several urban areas, proving that these markets are quite adaptive to social, economic and technological changes. The present study reveals that periodic marketing is an ecologically suitable commercial activity from the point of view of sustainable development because of the following reasons:

(1) The time involved in these markets is very short (only few hours) and periodicity is weekly, therefore, their impact on environment is minimum, which is quickly recovered by the natural cycle.

(2) There are no permanent shops or other establishments in these markets, therefore, problems like space, parking, traffic, etc., are minimised in comparison to daily markets.

(3) The periodic marketing system is more suitable for agrarian society of this region, where farmers have small fields, limited production and limited wants.
(4) The commodity structure of these markets is a reflection of the local environment.
(5) The pattern of 'market shift' provides a spatial interaction in the region.
(6) The practice followed by mobile traders is beneficial to them because it involves lesser investment and more sales, which otherwise is not possible at one place.
(7) These markets also provide an opportunity of social interaction among rural masses at regular intervals, which is one of the reasons for their survival.
(8) This system is more suitable for the region under study where villages are small in size and are located in a widespread area.
(9) Periodic markets have become an integral part of the cultural ecology of the region, therefore, their importance is growing in the region.

A point against weekly markets can be raised that on market days a large gathering disturbs the normal life and creates noise and air pollution. This is true but the duration of such gathering is barely four to five hours and during this short duration the adverse impact on environment is limited and is recovered through natural processes. With the help of district and local authority a few new centres of weekly markets be developed in areas where their number is limited. The suggested sites are Bapaur, Rajgarh, Khajuri in Sangod tehsil; Borabas and Dolia in Ladpura tehsil; and Khatali, Dhipri and Ohanwa in Piplod tehsil. During the first few months their importance and functioning be explained to people in order to develop an awareness of the benefits of these markets. When successful, these markets will help in rural development as well as in generating employment opportunities. In brief, for sustainable marketing development in rural areas, emphasis should be given on proper functioning of the existing periodic markets and steps should be taken for their further growth.

There is a need to prepare a 'master plan' for the development of marketing in market towns. This plan should be prepared keeping in view the present infrastructure and future projections for the next 25 years. In this plan emphasis should be given to selection of suitable sites for market-places. The selection of site for retail markets, shopping centres, agricultural *mandi*, warehouses, wholesale markets, parking places, etc., be made with the consideration of local environmental conditions. The interest of the consumers should be safeguarded. The present study can provide a base for such planning for Kota city. Immediate steps should be taken because unplanned growth of market-places has given rise to many problems responsible for the degradation of the urban environment. For 'agricultural *mandi*' development a separate master plan should be prepared. This master plan should be used for: (i) selection of new sites for the establishment of regulated markets, (ii) development of market infrastructure, (iii) improvement in functioning, and (iv) identification of areas in which the *mandi* committee can play a positive role in socio-economic development of the region.

The present study not only explains the role of ecological factors in growth and development of marketing system and/or market centres in the Central Hadaoti region but also suggests plans for sustainable development. There is a need for an integrated approach in planning of the marketing activities. The suggestions given above for the sustainable development of marketing will definitely provide a base in formulating both short- and long-term plans.

Bibliography

Acharya, S.S. (1988), *Agricultural Production, Marketing and Price Policy in India*, Mittal Pub, Delhi.

--- & Agarwal, N.L. (1987), *Agricultural Marketing in India*, Oxford, New Delhi.

Agarwal, P.C. (1968), Weekly Market Size and Service Area in Baster District, M.P., *Indian Geographical Journal*, Vol. 43, pp.29-33.

Allix, A. (1922), The Geography of Fairs: Illustrated by Old World Examples, *Geographical Review*, Vol. 12, pp. 523-69.

Applebaum, W. (1959), *Marketing Geography in American Geography, Inventory and Prospects*, Syracuse University, pp. 245-51.

Belshaw, C.S. (1965), *Traditional Exchange and Modern Markets*, Prentice Hall.

Berry, B.J.L. (1963), *Commercial Structure and Commercial Blight*, University of Chicago, Department of Geography, Research Paper No. 85.

— (1967), *Geography of Market Centres and Retail Distributions*, Prentice-Hall, pp. 42-58.

Bromley, R.J. (1971), Markets in the Developing Countries: A Review, *Geography*, Vol. 56, pp. 124-32.

--- (1974), Inter-regional Marketing and Alternative Reform Strategies in Ecuador, *European Journal of Marketing*, Vol. No. 3, pp. 245-64.

— (1974), *Periodic Markets, Daily Markets and Fairs: A Bibliography*, Monash University Publications in Geography, No. 10.

--- and Symanski, R. (1974), Market-place Trade in Latin America, *Latin America Research Review*, Vol. 9, No. 3, pp. 3-38.

---- (1975), Periodic Market and Rural Development Policy, *Cambria*, Vol. 2, No. 2, pp. 155-64.

---- Symanski, R. and Good, C.M. (1975), The Rationale of Periodic Markets, *Annals of the Association of American Geographers*, Vol. 65.

---- (1979), *Periodic Markets, Daily Markets and Fairs:* A Bibliography Supplement to 1979, Centre for Development Studies, University College of Swansea, Swansea, U.K.

Carter, H. (1976), *The Study of Urban Geography*, Edward Arnold, pp. 171-256.

Clark, W.A.V. (1967), The Spatial Structure of Retail Functions in a New Zealand City, *New Zealand Geographer*, Vol. 23, pp. 23-33.

---- (1968), Consumer Travel Patterns and the Concept of Range, *Annals of the Association of American Geographers*, Vol. 58, pp. 386-96.

Davies, Ross L. (1976), *Marketing Geography*, Methuen, London.

Deshpande, C.D. (1941), Market Villages and Periodic Fairs of Bombay-Karnataka, *Indian Geographical Journal*, Vol. 16, No. 4, pp. 327-39.

Dixit, R.S. (1984), Market Cycles, *Indian Journal of Marketing Geography*; 2(2) pp. 102-105.

---- (1984), *Market Centers and their Spatial Development in Umland of Kanpur*, Kitab Mahal, Allahabad.

---- (1997), Development of Marketing Geography in India, *Geographical Review of India*, 59 (2), pp. 164-172.

Fagerland, V.G. and Smith, R.H.T. (1970), A Preliminary Map of Market Periodicities in Ghana, *The Journal of Developing Areas*, Vol. 4, No. 3333-38.

Garnier, B.J. (1966), *The Internal Structure of Retail Nucleations*, North-western Studies in Geography, XII, Evanaton.

---- and Delobez, A. (1979), *Geography of Marketing*, Longman, pp. 169-236.

Gedam, D.A. (1974), A Geographical Analysis of Fairs at Salbardi, *Indian Geographical Journal*, 45 (1), pp. 17-24.

Good, C.M. (1975), Periodic Markets and Travelling Traders in Uganda, *Geographical Review*, Vol. 65, pp. 49-72.

Gormsen, E. (1976), *Market Distribution, Systems*: Papers Submitted to the Symposium K-18 of the 23rd. IGC, Moscow, July 28-29, 1976,

Johannes Gutenberg University Mainzer Geographiche Studies, No. 10, Mainz.

--- and Smith, R.H.T. (eds.) (1982), *Market Place Exchange Systems: Empirical and Theoretical Studies*, Mainz.

Harriss, Barbara (1984), *State and Market*, Concept, New Delhi.

Hay, A.M. and Smith R.H.T. (1980), The Spatio-temporal Synchronization of Periodic Markets: A Re-examination, *The Canadian Geographer*, Vol. xxiv, No. 2, pp. 149-64.

Hess, C.F. (1966), Geographical Aspects of Consumer Behaviour in the Retail Service Area of Greater Alborg, *Geografisk Tidds Skrift*, Vol. 65, pp. 1-26.

Hill Polly and Smith, R.H.T. (1972), The Spatial and Temporal Synchronization of Periodic Markets: Evidence from Four Emirates in Northern Nigeria, *Economic Geography*, Vol. 48, pp. 345-55.

Hodder, B.W. (1961), Rural Periodic Day Markets in Part of Yorubaland, *Transactions of the Institute of British Geographers*, No. 29, pp. 194-59.

--- (1970), Traditional Markets in Developing Countries, pp. 106-9 in *21st IGC India 1968, Selected papers,* Vol. 2, Economic Geography, National Committee for Geography, Calcutta.

— and Roger, Lee (1974), *Economic Geography*, Methuen, London.

--- and Sinha, R.M. (1976), Fairs Around Calcutta, *Geographical Review of India*, Vol. 38, pp. 187-92.

ICRISAT (1985), *Agricultural Markets in Semi-Arid Tropics*, Proceedings of the International Workshop held at ICRISAT Centre, India.

Ishihara, H. (ed.) (1987), *Markets and Marketing in Rural Bangladesh*, Department of Geography, Nagoya University, Nagoya.

--- (ed.) (1988), *Markets and Marketing in South India,* Department of Geography, Nagoya University, Nagoya.

Jayshankar, D.C. (1979), Marketing as a Catalyst for Regional Development, *Proceedings of Indo-British Seminar*, Madras, Dec. 8-17.

Jana, M.M. (1986), Retail Centres in Lower Silabati Basin, *Geographical Review of India*, 48 (1), pp. 64-72.

Kelley, E.J. (1955), Retail Structure of Urban Economy, *Traffic Quarterly*, Vol. 7, pp. 411-30.

Kendall, H.M. (1936), Fairs and Markets in the Department of Gers, France, *Economic Geography*, Vol. 12, pp. 42-57.

Khan, W. (1967), Food Markets in Dacca City, *Oriental Geographer*, Vol. 7, pp. 125-39.

Krishnan, V. (1932), Fairs and Trade Centres of Madura and Ramnad District, *Journal of the Madras Geographical Association*, Vol. 7, No. 3, pp. 237-49.

--- (1940), Fairs, Festivals and Shandies in Trichy District, *Journal of Madras Geographical Association*, Vol. 15, No. 3, pp. 272-76.

Lakshmanan, T.R. and Hansen, W.G. (1965), A Retail Market Potential Model, *Journal of the American Institute of Planners*, pp. 314-43.

McIntyre, W.F. (1965), The Retail Pattern of Manila, *Geographical Review*, Vol.45, pp. 66-80.

McKim, Wayne (1972), The Periodic Market System in North-eastern Ghana, *Economic Geography*, Vol. 48, pp. 333-34.

Mukherji, A.B. (1957), The Bi-weekly Market at Modinagar, *Indian Geographer*, Vol. 2, No. 2, pp. 271-93.

Mulvihill, D.F. and Mulvihill R.C. (1976), *Geography of Marketing and Urban Growth,* Van Nostrand Reinhold, New York.

Murdie, R.A. (1965), Cultural Differences in Consumer Travel, *Economic Geography*, Vol. 41, pp. 24-29.

National Council of Applied Economic Research (1972), *Market Centres and Spatial Development*, NCAER, New Delhi.

Neale, W.C., Singh, M. and Singh Jaipal (1965), Kurali Market: A Report on the Economic Geography of Marketing in Northern Punjab, *Economic Development and Cultural Change*, Vol. 13, pp. 129-68.

Pattanaik, N. (1935), Study of the Weekly Market of Baupli, *Geographical Review of India*, Vol. 15, No. 1, pp. 19-31.

Proudfoot, M.J. (1937), City Retail Structure, *Economic Geography*, Vol. 13, p.425.

Purton, R.W. (1973), *Markets and Fairs*, Routledge Kegan Paul, London.

Rajgopal (1988), *Micro-Level Planning for Agricultural Marketing*, Renaissance Pub., Delhi.

Remond, E. Murphy, Vanace, J.E and Epstein (1955), Internal Structure of the CBD, *Economic Geography*, Vol.31, No.1, pp.21-46.

Riddell, J.B. (1974), Periodic Markets in Sierra-Leone, *Annals of the Association of American Geographers*, Vol. 65, pp. 541-48.

Saxena, H.M. (1972), A Geographical Study of the Fairs of Hadaoti Plateau, *Deccan Geographers*, Vol. 10, No. 1, pp. 65-69.

--- (1974), Kota: A Study in Market Morphology, *Geographical Review of India*, Vol.36, No.1, p.45-49.

--- (1975), *Geography of Transport and Market Centres: A Case Study of Hadaoti Plateau*, S. Chand & Co., New Delhi.

— (1979), Morphology of the Market Towns: Theoretical Aspects and A Case Study of Sriganganagar, *Geographical Outlook*, Vol.14, pp. 87-93.

--- (1981), Geographical Study of Market Towns in Rajasthan, Unpublished Project Report, ICSSR, New Delhi.

--- (1982), Rural Markets: A Perspective for Development, *Annals of the Association of Rajasthan Geographers*, Vol.II, pp. 31-34.

--- (1987), Morphological Form and Typology of Market Towns in Rajasthan, in Yadav, C.S. (ed.), *Morphology of Towns*, Concept, N.Delhi, pp.107-113.

— (1988), *Rural Markets and Development*, Rawat Publications, Jaipur.

— (1990), *Marketing Geography*, Rawat Publications, Jaipur.

Scott, P. (1970), Geography and Retailing, Hutchinson, London.

Sinha, S.M. (1965), The Stability Theory of Rural Central Place Development, *National Geographical Journal of India*, Vol. II Part I, pp. 13-21.

Skinner, G.W. (1964-65), Marketing and Social Structure in Rural China, *Journal of Asian Studies*, Vol. 24, pp. 3-43, 195-228, and 363-99.

Slater, C.C. (1976), Marketing: A Catalyst for Development, pp. 3-17 in Izraeli, D., Izraeli, D.N. and Mesissner, F. (eds.), *Marketing Systems for Developing Countries*, Vol. I of Proceedings of INCOMAS. John-Wiley, New York.

Smith, R.H.T. and Hay (1969), A Theory of Spatial Structure of Internal Trade in Under-Developed Countries, *Geographical Analysis*, Vol. 1, pp. 121-36.

---- (1978), *Periodic Markets, Hawkers and Traders in Africa, Asia and Latin America*, University of British Colombia, Vancouver.

---- (1979), Periodic Market-place and Periodic Marketing: Review and Prospect, *Progress in Human Geography*, Vol. 3, No. 4, pp. 471-505 and Vol. 4, No. 1, pp. 1-3.

Spencer, J.E. (1940), The Szechwan Village Fair, *Economic Geography*, Vol. 16, pp. 48-58.

Srivastava, H.O. (1980), Geography of Market Centres in Saryupar Plain, Unpublished Ph.D Dissertation, Gorakhpur University.

Srivastava, K.R. (1983), Periodic Markets and Central Places in Baghelkhand Region, Unpublished Ph.D. Dissertation, Jabalpur University.

Srivastava, V.K. (1971), Trade Centres in Upper Son Basin, *Research Journal of Gorakhpur University*, pp. 37-42.

---- (1976), Market Periodicity and Centrality: A Methodological Approach, Mainzer Geographische Studien, (10), pp. 33-38.

---- (1978), Theoretical Norms and Interpretation of Marketplace Participants' Behaviour, *National Geographer*, 13 (2), pp. 117-124.

---- (1987), *Geography of Marketing and Rural Development*, Inter-India, New Delhi.

— (ed.) (1988), *Commercial Activities and Rural Development in South Asia*, Concept, New Delhi.

Symanski, R. and Bromley, R. (1974), Market Development and Ecological Complex, *Professional Geographer*, Vol. 26, pp. 382-88.

Tamaskar, B.G. (1977), Periodic Marketing System in Medieval Maharashtra, *Geographical Review of India*, Vol. 39, No. 2, pp. 173-82.

Tarrant, J.R. (1967), A Classification of Shop Types, *Professional Geographer*, Vol 19, pp.179-83.

Thakur, B. (1968), Models of Intra-Urban Consumer Travel Behaviour, *Indian Geographical Studies*, 2, pp. 21-27.

Thorpo, D. and Rhodes, T.C. (1966), The Shopping Centres of the Tyneside Urban and Large Scale Grocery Retailing, *Economic Geography*, Vol.42, pp.52-73.

Vance, J.E. (1970), *The Merchant's World: The Geography of Wholesaling*, Prentice-Hall.

Verma, L.N. and Saxena, H.M (1968), Jhalaranpatan: A Geographical Study of a Market Centre, *Deccan Geographer*, Vol.6, No.2, July-December, p. 25.

Wanmali, S. (1980), The Regulated and Periodic Markets and Rural Development in India, *Transactions of IBG*, Vol. 5, No. 4, pp. 446-485.

Wrigley, G.M. (1919), Fairs of the Central Andes, *Geographical Review*, Vol. 7, pp. 65-80.

Yull, R.S. (1967), Spatial Behaviour of Retail Customers, Some Empirical Measurements, *Geografiska Annaler*, pp. 105-15.

Index

Therefore, it is clear that marketing activities in urban areas have their impact on the environment. In order to fulfil the demands of the growing population these activities keep increasing. Therefore, there is a need for sustainable development of market-places and other market infrastructure. In Central Hadaoti region immediate steps should be taken for Kota city and planning for other urban centres should be done.

Agricultural Marketing and its Impact on Environment

In the region under study all the marketing of agricultural products is done at 'Krishi Upaj Mandi' locally known as 'Dhan Mandi'. This *mandi* is not a separate entity but a part of urban or rural settlement. Sometimes the location of an agricultural *mandi* is amidst a residential area as in case of Ramganjmandi, Sumerganjmandi, Sangod and Old Kota Mandi, thus affecting adversely the local environment. Inside the *mandi* also some environmental problems have emerged. Due to heavy cart and tractor traffic the entire atmosphere of that area becomes dusty. Regular cleaning is never undertaken. The failure of the drainage system or the non-existence of it adds to the woes of the people there. During morning and evening hours, when arrival and departure of vehicles is at its peak, the approach roads become dusty and polluted. With the introduction of regulated marketing and construction of market yards, these problems have been minimised but more efforts in the direction are needed.

Impact of Rural Markets on Environment

As described in an earlier chapter rural markets play a vital role in the rural economy. In Central Hadaoti region rural marketing is performed by periodic marketing, i.e., weekly markets and fairs. There is a need to examine the environmental impact of weekly markets and fairs so that steps for sustainable marketing development can be taken for future planning.